I0007353

Microsoft Dynamics CRM 2011 New Features

Get up to speed with the new features of Microsoft Dynamics CRM 2011

Jim Wang

Darren Liu

BIRMINGHAM - MUMBAI

Microsoft Dynamics CRM 2011 New Features

Copyright © 2011 Packt Publishing

All rights reserved. No part of this book may be reproduced, stored in a retrieval system, or transmitted in any form or by any means, without the prior written permission of the publisher, except in the case of brief quotations embedded in critical articles or reviews.

Every effort has been made in the preparation of this book to ensure the accuracy of the information presented. However, the information contained in this book is sold without warranty, either express or implied. Neither the authors, nor Packt Publishing, and its dealers and distributors will be held liable for any damages caused or alleged to be caused directly or indirectly by this book.

Packt Publishing has endeavored to provide trademark information about all of the companies and products mentioned in this book by the appropriate use of capitals. However, Packt Publishing cannot guarantee the accuracy of this information.

First published: November 2011

Production Reference: 1281011

Published by Packt Publishing Ltd.
Livery Place
35 Livery Street
Birmingham B3 2PB, UK.

ISBN 978-1-84968-206-0

www.packtpub.com

Cover Image by Artie Ng (artherng@yahoo.com.au)

Credits

Authors
Jim Wang
Darren Liu

Reviewers
Harry Riddle
Sandor Schellenberg
Ankit Shah

Acquisition Editor
Amey Kanse

Development Editor
Susmita Panda

Technical Editor
Snehal Gawde

Project Coordinator
Vishal Bodwani

Proofreader
Dirk Manuel

Indexer
Hemangini Bari

Graphics
Nilesh Mohite

Production Coordinator
Arvindkumar Gupta

Cover Work
Arvindkumar Gupta

About the Authors

Jim Wang is specialized in enterprise solution at CSC Microsoft Practice, in UK; He focuses on consulting, solutioning, and developing on the Microsoft Dynamics CRM, SharePoint, and Office365/Cloud platforms.

Jim has been awarded the Microsoft Most Valuable Professional (MVP) on Dynamics CRM for 4 years, with full lifecycle knowledge of the product. He has great interest in mobile technologies, ALM (Application Lifecycle Management), and Agile methodologies, with extensive and focused experience in Microsoft technologies. Jim was also recognized as a British Computer Society Chartered IT Professional (CITP) in 2009.

Jim is a co-founder of the official Microsoft Dynamics CRM Chinese community, which aims to help partners and customers to develop and use Dynamics CRM in the Greater China Region.

His blog, `http://jianwang.blogspot.com`, is one of the most visited blogs about Microsoft Dynamics CRM.

Acknowledgement

I would like to thank the guys at Packt Publishing for giving me the opportunity to write this book.

Special thanks go to Amey Kanse for believing in this project, and to Vishal Bodwani, and Susmita Panda, along with the technical reviewers: Ankit Shah, Harry Riddle, Sandor Schellenberg, and Snehal Gawde for dealing with my drafts and giving feedbacks.

A big "thank you" goes to my dear friend, the co-author of this book: Darren Liu, who has spent weekends with me discussing and writing the book efficiently.

I would also mention the Microsoft Dynamics CRM community, and its former leader, Jim Glass, who retired from Microsoft as this book was being finalized. Thanks so much for their generous support while I was writing this book.

Finally, I want to thank my wife Jin and our upcoming baby Michelle, for being patient while I was writing the book over many weekends. I'd like to thank my parents too, for sometimes ignoring them while I was writing the book.

Finally, thank you very much for reading the book. If you have any questions, please let us know.

Darren Liu, Microsoft CRM MVP alumni and Certified Microsoft CRM Professional, has been working with Dynamics CRM since version 1.0. After joining Microsoft in 2009, his primary focus has been solution architecture, data migration, and system integration. Darren has been engaged on many enterprise CRM projects and played many different important roles throughout his career. Today, Darren is playing a key role as solution architect/development team lead working on a global biotech Dynamics CRM implementation. This has involved the typical key activities of a project lifecycle of coordinating with the key business sponsors, gathering requirements, design, proof of concept delivery, development, testing, documentation, and support.

Darren is a co-founder of the official Microsoft Dynamics CRM Chinese community, forums, and several newsgroups that aim to help partners, customers, and individuals. He has also been a speaker and trainer for Microsoft, training partners in the Greater China region.

Darren can be reached at `Darren.Liu@microsoft.com`.

I would like to thank my wife, Min, for supporting me during the writing of this book. She took care of our two-year old son while I was writing. I would like to thank my parents for babysitting my son whenever we asked. Writing this book required a great amount of time away from my normal work responsibilities. I have spent many nights and weekends working on it, but my family has supported me from start to finish. I would like to thank my mentor, Darren Hubert, for his support and also for giving me opportunities to work on enterprise projects as a lead, where I gained skills in many different areas. Special thanks to Packt Publishing for giving us the opportunity to work on this book.

Lastly, I would like to thank my good friend, the co-author of this book, Jim Wang, who has helped me to revise and to proofread the chapters that I wrote. I would also like to thank him for spending many nights and weekends, in the past year, working on this book with me.

About the Reviewers

Sandor Schellenberg is the owner and founder of friendlyITsolutions, which mainly focuses on Microsoft Dynamics CRM and related software in the Microsoft stack. He is a Senior Microsoft Dynamics CRM Consultant/Solution Architect and is specialized in data migration and integration.

In autumn 2009, his work was recognized and rewarded with an invitation to the Scribe Software MVP Program, and in spring 2011, Sandor was reselected for this program.

His roots in Microsoft-based Internet technologies go back more than fourteen years, and since 2005 he has specialized in Microsoft Dynamics CRM. Following his first guest post on the blog of Menno te Koppele, he decided to start his own blog, Friendly Microsoft CRM Monster — a blog with a wink. The blog is widely-read in the Dynamics CRM community, and is focused mainly on Microsoft Dynamics CRM technical and integration/migration topics. He is also the author of several 'musings' at `msdynamics.com`, where he writes about common topics that have to be faced during implementations of Dynamics CRM.

He has experience in implementing Dynamics CRM in several branches and companies in the small-to-midsize segment, as well as in the enterprise segment. His experience in migrations and integrations is not only within the Microsoft stack, but also with widely-used software from other vendors, including Oracle and SAP.

Ankit Shah is a highly-motivated and experienced professional, holding a Bachelor Science in Information Technology — B.Sc. (I.T.), and securing 7+ years of IT experience in software design and development. Presently Ankit is working as a Dynamics CRM consultant at Inkey Solutions, Surat, India. He has seen most of the stages of the Software Development Life Cycle (SDLC), and is a committed individual with high moral values, a positive attitude, and integrity. He has worked on Microsoft Technologies like MS CRM 3.0, 4.0 and 2011 online/on premises/ offline, Silverlight 3.0/4.0, WPF, WCF, C# 4.0, ASP .Net, AJAX, JavaScript, XML Web Services, Microsoft Application Blocks, SQL Server 2005/2008, and various source controls such as VSS, TFS 2008/2010, Clear Case, and Rational XDE.Net.

Prior to joining Inkey Solutions, Ankit has worked with Accenture, Patni, and JZERO PVT. LTD.

www.PacktPub.com

Support files, eBooks, discount offers and more

You might want to visit www.PacktPub.com for support files and downloads related to your book.

Did you know that Packt offers eBook versions of every book published, with PDF and ePub files available? You can upgrade to the eBook version at www.PacktPub.com and as a print book customer, you are entitled to a discount on the eBook copy. Get in touch with us at service@packtpub.com for more details.

At www.PacktPub.com, you can also read a collection of free technical articles, sign up for a range of free newsletters and receive exclusive discounts and offers on Packt books and eBooks.

http://PacktLib.PacktPub.com

Do you need instant solutions to your IT questions? PacktLib is Packt's online digital book library. Here, you can access, read and search across Packt's entire library of books.

Why Subscribe?
- Fully searchable across every book published by Packt
- Copy and paste, print and bookmark content
- On demand and accessible via web browser

Free Access for Packt account holders

If you have an account with Packt at www.PacktPub.com, you can use this to access PacktLib today and view nine entirely free books. Simply use your login credentials for immediate access.

Instant Updates on New Packt Books

Get notified! Find out when new books are published by following @PacktEnterprise on Twitter, or the *Packt Enterprise* Facebook page.

Table of Contents

Preface

Microsoft Dynamics CRM 2011 offers exciting new features that enable you to build and maintain a robust customer relationship management system for your organization.

This book is your one-stop resource for getting grips with most of the new features of Dynamics CRM 2011. To make learning fun and engaging, we will build an Airline Compensation Management (ACM) demo system using Dynamics CRM 2011.

This book starts by setting up the development environment for Microsoft Dynamics CRM 2011. Then it walks through building a structural architecture for the ACM system and configuring it in Dynamics CRM 2011. In the process, the book describes the new customization features offered by Dynamics CRM 2011.

In addition, this book covers SharePoint integration with CRM, Charts and Dashboards, customizing the CRM Ribbon and Site Map, and to show you how to extend Dynamics CRM 2011 in the Cloud.

What this book covers

Chapter 1, Setting Up the Development Workspace, shows how to set up and configure a Microsoft Dynamics CRM 2011 development workspace that you can use for the project.

Chapter 2, System Design and Configuration, gives you a high level overview of an Airline Compensation Management (ACM) XRM application that we are going to build in Microsoft Dynamics CRM 2011.

Chapter 3, Data Import, populates some sample data into Microsoft Dynamics CRM 2011 for testing and further development, using new Import Data Wizard.

Chapter 4, Client-Side Programming, gives you an overview of the new client-side programming features in Microsoft Dynamics CRM 2011.

Chapter 5, Server-Side Programming, introduces the Microsoft Dynamics CRM 2011 event-driven, server-side programming methods: Plug-ins and Processes.

Chapter 6, SharePoint Integration, guides you through how to enable and configure the SharePoint integration feature in Microsoft Dynamics CRM 2011.

Chapter 7, Charts and Dashboards, covers the new business intelligence features of Microsoft Dynamics CRM 2011, such as Filters, Charts, and Dashboards.

Chapter 8, Extending Microsoft Dynamics CRM 2011 in the Cloud, introduces Microsoft cloud offerings, and sets up a portal site on the Windows Azure platform and integrates this portal with Microsoft Dynamics CRM 2011 Online.

Chapter 9, Sitemap and Ribbon Customization, covers customization of the Sitemap and the Ribbon.

Chapter 10, Packaging It Up, explains solutions, and how to better use them to help us deploy our customizations into different environments.

What you need for this book

Because this book covers the new features of Microsoft Dynamics CRM 2011, you should have a good knowledge of configurating and customizing Microsoft Dynamics CRM 4.0. Because we'll be using Dynamics CRM Online and Windows Azure to configure and to customize the ACM system, you will need a Windows Live ID. You may sign up for a Live ID at https://signup.live.com/signup.aspx.

Who this book is for

We wrote this book for professionals who want to get up-to-speed with the new features of Microsoft Dynamics CRM 2011.

Conventions

In this book, you will find a number of styles of text that distinguish between different kinds of information. Here are some examples of these styles, and an explanation of their meaning.

Code words in text are shown as follows: "the template is in an XML Spreadsheet 2003 format, with an .xml extension".

A block of code is set as follows:

```
<EntityMaps>
  <EntityMap TargetEntityName="acm_airport"
    SourceEntityName="Airport" Dedupe="Eliminate"
    ProcessCode="Process"/>
  <EntityMap TargetEntityName="acm_flightroute"
    SourceEntityName="Flight Route" Dedupe="Eliminate"
    ProcessCode="Process"/>
</EntityMaps>
```

New terms and **important words** are shown in bold. Words that you see on the screen, in menus or dialog boxes for example, appear in the text like this: "run **Windows Update** and take a snapshot at this stage".

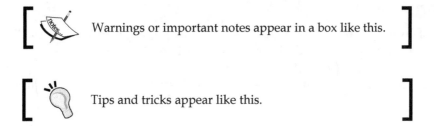

Warnings or important notes appear in a box like this.

Tips and tricks appear like this.

Reader feedback

Feedback from our readers is always welcome. Let us know what you think about this book—what you liked or may have disliked. Reader feedback is important for us to develop titles that you really get the most out of.

To send us general feedback, simply send an e-mail to feedback@packtpub.com, and mention the book title via the subject of your message.

If there is a book that you need and would like to see us publish, please send us a note in the **SUGGEST A TITLE** form on www.packtpub.com or e-mail suggest@packtpub.com.

If there is a topic that you have expertise in and you are interested in either writing or contributing to a book, see our author guide on www.packtpub.com/authors.

Customer support

Now that you are the proud owner of a Packt book, we have a number of things to help you to get the most from your purchase.

Errata

Although we have taken every care to ensure the accuracy of our content, mistakes do happen. If you find a mistake in one of our books — maybe a mistake in the text or the code — we would be grateful if you would report this to us. By doing so, you can save other readers from frustration and help us improve subsequent versions of this book. If you find any errata, please report them by visiting http://www.packtpub.com/support, selecting your book, clicking on the **errata submission form** link, and entering the details of your errata. Once your errata are verified, your submission will be accepted and the errata will be uploaded on our website, or added to any list of existing errata, under the Errata section of that title. Any existing errata can be viewed by selecting your title from http://www.packtpub.com/support.

Piracy

Piracy of copyright material on the Internet is an ongoing problem across all media. At Packt, we take the protection of our copyright and licenses very seriously. If you come across any illegal copies of our works, in any form, on the Internet, please provide us with the location address or website name immediately so that we can pursue a remedy.

Please contact us at copyright@packtpub.com with a link to the suspected pirated material.

We appreciate your help in protecting our authors, and our ability to bring you valuable content.

Questions

You can contact us at questions@packtpub.com if you are having a problem with any aspect of the book, and we will do our best to address it.

1
Setting Up the Development Workspace

The first step in this project is to set up a workspace, so you can build, test, and verify all of the components that we are going to put together in Microsoft Dynamics CRM 2011 for our Airline Compensation Management system. In this chapter, we would like to show you how to set up and configure a development workspace that you can use for the project. Hence, we will cover the following topics:

- System requirements
- Workstation requirements
- Virtualization options
- Setting up Microsoft Hyper-V on the Workstation
- Setting up Server Environment on the VM
- Setting up SharePoint 2010
- Setting up Microsoft Dynamics CRM 2011
- Setting up Development Tools

System requirements

Microsoft Dynamics CRM Server 2011 and SharePoint Server 2010 require certain hardware and several software applications that work together. We are going to install and set up all of the components for our development workspace in a single virtual image.

Before setting up Microsoft Dynamics CRM and SharePoint Server for your production environment, please refer to the Implementation Guide for hardware and software requirements for each of the products.

Hardware requirements

Microsoft Dynamics CRM Server 2011 requires 64-bit hardware.

The following table lists the minimum and recommended hardware requirements for a Microsoft Dynamics CRM server running in a Full Server configuration. These requirements assume that additional components, such as Microsoft SQL Server, Microsoft SQL Server Reporting Services, Microsoft SharePoint, and Microsoft Exchange Server are not currently installed or running on the system.

Components	Minimum	Recommended
Processor	x64 architecture or compatible dual-core 1.5 GHz processor	Quad-core x64 architecture 2 GHz CPU or higher such as AMD Opteron or Intel Xeon systems
Memory	2 GB RAM	8 GB RAM or more
Hard disk	10 GB of available hard disk space	40 GB or more of available hard disk space

Because we will have SharePoint Server 2010 installed on the same virtual image, it requires at least 4 GB RAM and a Duo-core x64 architecture 2 GHz CPU to run both server products smoothly. Alternatively, you may install SharePoint Foundation 2010 instead of SharePoint Server 2010, for better performance.

Software requirements

Microsoft Dynamics CRM Server 2011 must be installed on a 64-bit operating system. The following table lists the supported software requirements for CRM and SharePoint:

Components	Supported
Operating System	Windows Server 2008 (x64), Standard, Enterprise, Datacenter, Web Server, Small Business Server Standard or Small Business Server Premium edition, with SP2 or a later version

Components	Supported
SQL Server and Reporting Services	Microsoft SQL Server 2008 (x64), Standard, Enterprise, Datacenter or Developer edition, with SP1 or a later version
Internet Information Services (IIS)	IIS 7.0 or a later version, in Native Mode
Active Directory modes	Windows 2000 Mixed or Native, Windows 2003 Interim or Native, Windows 2008 Interim or Native
.Net Version	ASP .NET 4.0
Software Component Prerequisites	SQL Server Agent service, SQL Server Full Text Indexing, Indexing Service, IIS Admin, World Wide Web Publishing, and Windows Data Access Components (MDAC) 6.0

 For more details about the Microsoft Dynamics CRM Server 2011 hardware and software requirements, please visit `http://technet.microsoft.com/en-us/library/gg554695.aspx`.

Workstation requirements

You do need a powerful workstation in order to run the virtualized environment smoothly. The recommended configuration is as follows:

- Processor: Intel Core Duo CPU
- Memory: At least 4 GB RAM; recommended 8GB RAM
- Hard disk: At least 40 GB or more of available hard disk space
- Internet Access: Wireless and/or Cable adaptor
- Operating System: 64-bit Windows Server 2008 R2 or Windows 7

In addition to the system requirements for Windows Server 2008 R2 as described in the release notes, a 64-bit system with hardware-assisted virtualization enabled and data execution prevention (DEP) is required. It is also recommended to ensure that you have a clean install of x64 edition of Windows Server 2008 R2 to be able to use the Hyper-V technology.

 A VHD file can be used in both VirtualBox and Hyper-V.

Virtualization options

Microsoft Dynamics CRM Server 2011 and SharePoint Server 2010 can be deployed in a virtualized environment. You have several options for your virtualization solutions from different vendors. However, please understand the limitations of using a virtualized environment before you use them in your production environments. We will set up the CRM development workspace in a single VM image (Virtual Machine image) that is running on the workstation. The following table lists the three different virtual products that you can use to set up the development workspace on your host computer:

Software	Vendor	License
Microsoft Hyper-V	Microsoft	Free with Windows Server
VMware Server 2	VMware	Free
VirtualBox	Oracle	Free

In this book, we choose to use Microsoft Hyper-V running on a 64-bit Windows Server 2008 R2 Standard Edition. For more information about Hyper-V, please see the Microsoft Virtualization website at `http://www.microsoft.com/virtualization/en/us/default.aspx`.

If you are running Windows 7, you may set up the development workspace by using VirtualBox, which also supports 64-bit Guest OS and a VHD (virtual hard disk). You can create a VHD by using the Disk Management tool in Windows 7 (go to **Start** | **Run**: type in `diskmgmt.msc` and press *Enter*, then select **Action** | **Create VHD**).

Setting up Microsoft Hyper-V

To set up Hyper-V on your Windows Server 2008 Workstation, please follow these steps:

1. Install the Hyper-V server role on the workstation:

   - **Start** | **Run**..., type in "ServerManager.msc" and press *Enter*.
   - Right-click **Roles** and then select **Add Roles**.
   - Select **Hyper-V** and then click **Next** and then **Install**.

2. Create two Virtual Network connections that allow a remote desktop connection from the workstation to the VM:

    *   Open Hyper-V manager, select the **Virtual Network Manager…** on the **Action** menu, add two **Virtual Networks** as per the following table, and then click **OK**.

Name	Connection Type
External—Virtual Network	External (with your network connection)
Internal—Virtual Network	Internal only

    *   Hyper-V will create two new network connections. Go to **Control Panel | Network and Internet | Network Connections**, and rename the connections to:
        *   Hyper-V External Connection
        *   Hyper-V Internal Connection

3. Set up the Internet access via a wireless network:

    *   Out of the box, Hyper-V doesn't support Internet access via the wireless network. We need to create a wireless network connection in order for VM to access the Internet.

    *   Go to **Control Panel | Network and Internet | Network Connections**, and select both **Hyper-V Internal Connection** and your **Wireless Network Connection**, right-click and select **Bridge Connections**. This will create a Network Bridge between the workstation and VM, which allows Internet access via the workstation's wireless connection.

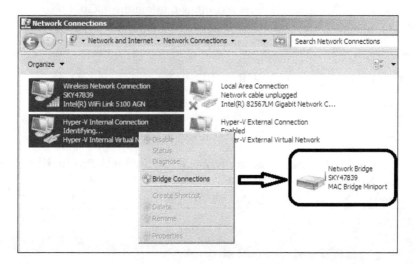

Setting up the Server Environment on the VM

We need to create a new VM image, and then install and configure Windows server and SQL server on the VM.

Windows Server 2008 R2 and SQL Server 2008 R2 installation

Please follow the below steps to set up VM, and install Windows Server and SQL Server:

1. Create a new VM for Microsoft Dynamics CRM 2011 server:

   - Open the Hyper-V manager, and then select **New | Virtual Machine...** from the **Action** menu:

Name and Location	Name: CRM 2011 Location: D:\Hyper-V\
Assign Memory	Depends on your total memory; recommend minimum 4 GB.
Configure Networking	Hyper-V Internal Virtual Network. Hyper-V External Virtual Network. (In **Settings | Add Hardware | Network Adapter**).
Connect Virtual Hard Disk	Create a virtual hard disk: Name: CRM 2011.vhd, Location: D:\Hyper-V\, Size: recommend minimum 40GB.
Installation Options	Select a path to the Windows Server 2008 R2 drive or ISO image.

2. Install the guest OS on the CRM 2011 VM:

Operating System	Windows Server 2008 R2 Enterprise Edition.
Server Name	Rename the server on the 1st start.
	Server Name: **BPS (Business Productivity Server)**. You may choose your server name.
Domain Name	XRM.LOCAL (run: dcpromo.exe).

Server Roles	Active Directory Domain Services, Application Server, DNS Server, Web Server (IIS).
Enable Remote Desktop connection on VM	This allows you to share data between VM and HOST.
Domain Administrator account	Account: xrm\Administrator.

3. Install SQL Server 2008 R2:

Instance Features	Database Engine Services, SQL Server Replication, Full-Text Search, Reporting Services, Management Tools.
Run as Service Account	Run Active Directory Users and Computers (dsa. msc), then go to **Users**, right-click on the Administrator account, select **Copy**, and then create a new administrator account: xrm\AdminService. Open the account, change the **Account** option to **Password never expires**, and then use this account to run SQL services.
Authentication Mode	Windows authentication mode.
Reporting Services Configuration	Native mode default configuration.

4. Now we have a Windows Server 2008 R2 + SQL Server 2008 R2 workspace. Please validate the installation by checking the system event log: Go to **Start | Run...**, type in "eventvwr" and press *Enter*, then check the **Administrative Events** and correct any errors.

5. Run **Windows Update** and take a snapshot at this stage:

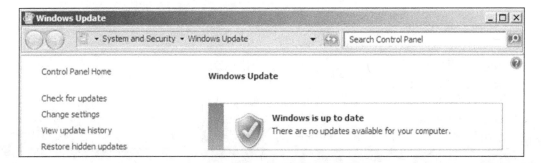

Setting up SharePoint 2010

Install and configure SharePoint Server on the VM. Create a new site collection called CRM Document Workspace.

Installing SharePoint 2010 Server

1. Install KB979917 — QFE for Sharepoint issues — Perf Counter fix & User Impersonation.

2. Run the SharePoint installation file, and follow the wizard to install the software prerequisites first, and then install the SharePoint Server:

Configuration Database Server	BPS
Configuration Database Name	SharePoint_Config
Database Access Account	xrm\AdminService
Specify port number	2010
Authentication Provider	NTLM

Creating a SharePoint web application that supports both Windows and Claims Based Authentication

1. Create a new Web Application:

Authentication	Claims Based Authentication
IIS Web Site	SharePoint-6666
Port	6666
Host Header	<empty>
Path	`C:\inetpub\wwwroot\wss\VirtualDirectories\6666`
Allow Anonymous	No
Use Secure Sockets Layer (SSL)	No
Enable Windows Authentication	Yes
Integrated Windows authentication	NTLM
Sign In Page URL	Default Sign In Page
URL	`http://BPS:6666`

Application Pool	Create a new application pool: SharePoint-6666
	Run as account: xrm\AdminService
Database Server	BPS
Database Name	WSS_Content
Database Authentication	Windows authentication
Service Application Connections	default

2. Create a Site Collection:

Title	CRM Document Workspace
URL	`http://BPS:6666`
Template	Document Workspace
Primary Site Collection Administrator	xrm\Administrator
Secondary Site Collection Administrator	Administrator@xrm.local

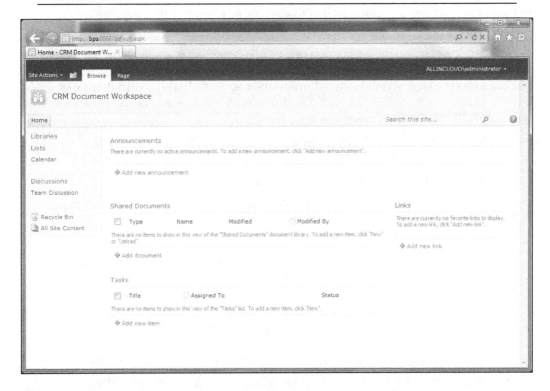

Setting up Microsoft Dynamics CRM 2011

There are different options for setting up Dynamics CRM for your development workspace. Microsoft Dynamics CRM Online provides a quick way for you to get a CRM instance running without installing any hardware or software, so that you can focus more on your project tasks. On the other hand, Microsoft Dynamics CRM On-Premise allows you to control where to install the application and where to store your data. This makes integration with your existing application much simpler than CRM Online. Both have their pros and cons; you may select the option that makes the most sense for your organization.

For development purposes, you can develop a CRM Online solution in an On-Premise development workspace, and then import the solution to CRM Online.

Microsoft Dynamics CRM On-Premise

Because we are building a CRM environment for our development workspace, just to keep it simple, we are going to install and configure CRM in a standalone virtual server.

To perform a fresh install of Microsoft Dynamics CRM, follow these steps:

1. Log on to the server with a domain user account that has administrator-level privileges to Active Directory and that is also a member of the Administrator group on the local computer.

2. Navigate to the folder that contains the Microsoft Dynamics CRM installation files.

3. Click on **SetupServer.exe** to start the installation.

4. On the **Welcome to Microsoft Dynamics CRM Setup** page, click **Next** to move to the next step.

Note: It is recommended to get the latest installation file for Microsoft Dynamics CRM; however it is not required.

5. On the **Product Key Information** page, enter your product key (you can use the MSDN/TechNet Plus license if you are a subscriber, or you can use the 90-day trail key) in the product key boxes, and then click **Next** to continue.

6. Accept the **License Agreement** by selecting the **I accept this license agreement** checkbox, and then click **Next** to continue.

Note: Dynamics CRM 2011 detects the missing required components and it will display them in the **Install Required Components** page. You must install the missing components prior to moving to the next step. If you have already installed all required components, the **Install Required Component** page will not appear.

7. Browse to the location into which you want to install CRM on the **Select Installation Location** page. Select **Full Server** on the **Specify Server Roles** page, because we are installing it in a single virtual server image. Click **Next** to continue.

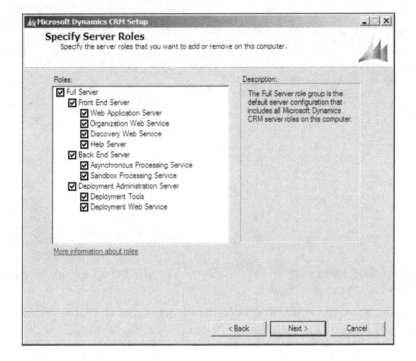

8. On the **Specify Deployment Options** page, select **Create a new deployment option**.
9. Select the required instance of SQL server, and then click **Next** to continue.
10. On the **Select the Organization Unit** page, select the location into which you want the CRM organization unit to be installed, and then click **Next** to continue.

 Note: It is recommended to create a new **Organization Unit** in **Active Directory** for CRM.

11. On the **Specify Security Account** page, select the **Security account** for the Microsoft CRM services and ASP.NET components, and then click **Next** to continue.

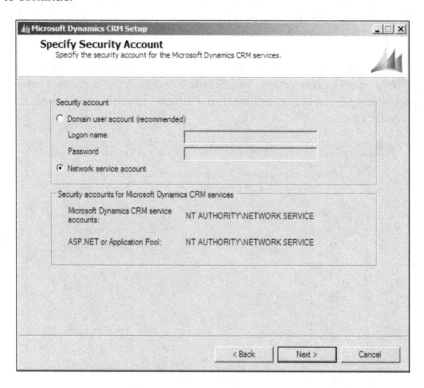

12. Select the **Create a new Web Site** option on the **Select a Web Site** page, and then click **Next** to continue.

13. On the **Specify E-mail Router Setting** page, enter the **server name** where the **E-mail Router** is installed, and then click **Next** to continue.

 Note: You may leave the **E-mail Router** box blank. However, if you decide to install the E-mail router later, you have to add the computer where the E-mail Router is installed to the PrivUserGroup in Active Directory.

14. On the **Specifiy the Organization Name** page, enter the **Display Name**, select the **Currency** and **Base Language** for your organization, and then click **Next** to continue.

15. On the **Specify Reporting Services Server** page, enter the **Report Server URL** and then click **Next** to continue.

16. On the **Help Us Improve the Customer Experience** page, select whether you want to participate in the **Customer Experience Improvement Program** and then click **Next** to continue. When everything passes the **System Checks** (as shown below) click **Next** to continue.

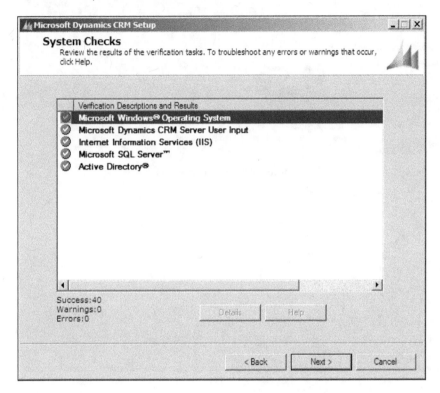

17. Review the **Ready to Install Microsoft Dynamics CRM** page, and then click **Install** to start the installation of Dynamics CRM.

18. When the setup completes successfully, the **Microsoft Dynamics Server setup completed** page appears. Select the **Launch Microsoft Dynamics CRM Reporting Extensions Setup** checkbox, and then follow the wizard to complete the installation.

19. Click **Finish** to complete the installation. Now that the server has been installed, try browsing the server at `http://bps`; you will see the default **Microsoft Dynamics CRM 2011** user interface, as shown in the following screenshot:

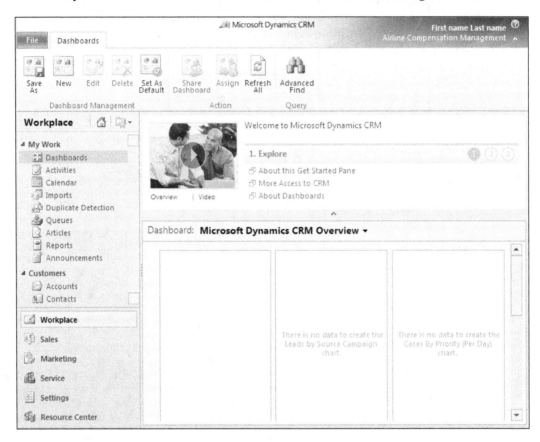

20. After installing CRM, check the event log: Go to **Start** | **Run**, type in "eventvwr" and press *Enter*. Expand **Event Viewer** | **Custom Views** | **Administrative Events**. If you see any errors, please fix them before continuing.

You might see an Error Event 17203, MSCRMTracing – Invalid Trace Directory.

That's because CRM has a default trace output directory: `c:\crmdrop\logs`, that doesn't exist. You can fix this error by creating the folder structure and granting permission to the Network Services account.

For more information about CRM tracing, please visit KB907490 - How to enable tracing in Microsoft Dynamics CRM: `http://support.microsoft.com/kb/907490`.

Setting up Development Tools

To complete this task, you will also need to install Visual Studio 2010. You can download a trial version of Visual Studio 2010 from `http://www.microsoft.com/visualstudio/en-us/try`.

Visual Studio 2010 can be either installed in VM, or install on your host computer for better performance and manageability. More details about setting up Visual Studio on the Host computer and enable remote debugging, please visit Jim Wang's blog: `http://jianwang.blogspot.com/2011/07/crm-2011-plugin-development-workspace.html`.

> Because Visual Studio 2010 does not support the Integration Services, Report Services and Analysis Services projects for SQL Server 2008/R2. If you are developing CRM reports, you need the Visual Studio 2008 or Business Intelligence Development Studio (an optional component in the SQL Server 2008/R2 installation), as well as the Microsoft Dynamics CRM 2011 Report Authoring Extension.

Summary

In this chapter, we have covered how to set up your development workspace for this project. You have several options for setting up your development workspace, Dynamics CRM 2011 and SharePoint 2010; consider choosing the option that makes the most sense for your organization.

2
System Design and Configuration

In this chapter, we are going to walk you through an Airline Compensation Management (ACM) system solution in Microsoft Dynamics CRM 2011. During this walkthrough, we would like to show the new and improved features of CRM 2011. You need to understand the requirements to build a good solution.

- Vision and scope
- ACM system overview
- System architectural design
- Defining the ACM Data model
- Configuring the ACM system
- ACM system security structure

Airline Compensation Management system

Air-X is an international scheduled airline company that is engaged in the passenger airline transportation business. Its principal activities consist of the provision of domestic and international airline services.

Air-X has over 10,000 employees globally; the company flies to more than 100 destinations worldwide. Air-X prides itself on their employee-care culture, together with their customer-care mission. The ACM system initiative is a part of the Air-X's Employee-Care platform, which has strong extensible capabilities and an intuitive user-experience.

Vision and scope

Air-X would like to replace their outdated crew compensation system. The existing system was not able to show how the compensations are composed; some of the business processes required manual input of data which created more work for the administrative team and lead to inaccurate payouts to the employees. The Air-X management team and the crews would like to have a complete view of all of the flight activities and how each employee is going to get compensated. They came up with the following vision statement for this project:

> *"To create an advanced system that provides a 360 degrees view of all of the employees, flight activities and compensation information in order to improve accuracy and efficiency. To implement a system that is easy to use by the employees, easy to maintain by the Information Technology team, and that provides capabilities for expansion in order to satisfy the future business needs."*

In addition to their vision, they have identified the following requirements:

- The system shall store the crew members, contact information, flight activities, and compensation.
- The system shall store the flight route, flight, and airport information.
- The system shall provide a way to capture feedback on the system.
- The system shall allow crew members to log on to the system via the Internet.
- The system shall allow crew members to see their monthly compensation details.
- The system shall allow the airline scheduler to the update crew members' flight schedule.
- The system shall provide reports to the management team to allow them to see the compensation for and performance of crew members.
- The system shall allow the import of existing data from the legacy systems.
- The system shall allow integration with external systems.
- The system shall use the Microsoft technologies, as all of the current systems are using Microsoft technology stacks.

Based on the requirements above, the Air-X team has identified Microsoft Dynamics CRM 2011 as a great fit for them, because it can be integrated perfectly due to the xRM capabilities.

 Note: Compensation is the remuneration received by a flight attendant in return for his/her contribution to the Airline Company.

The scope for this project is to implement the Microsoft Dynamics CRM 2011 with a well-defined system customization for the initial taste. As well as to provide a integrated Crew Portal prototype in order to the further development. Integration of the current system is out of scope, and will be discussed in the next phase.

ACM system overview

The Airline Compensation Management (ACM) system is to keep track of the compensation for the crew members. Each crew member is compensated differently based on their level and the length of their flight segments, so his or her compensation is composed of the basic salary, hourly pay, and the per diem for the layover in locations other than their base location.

Each crew member gets a basic salary per month. In addition to their basic salary, each crew member gets paid extra based on the number of hours they spend on the actual flight. The amount per hour is based on their level. For example, Crew Level 1's hourly payment is $5.00 and Crew Level 2's payment is $6.00, and so on... Crew members also get a per diem for each hour that they stay in a location other than their base location. For example, assume that a crew member's base location is London; if she flies to Chicago and stays for 10 hours, then she will get an extra $100.00 compensation, assuming the per diem for Chicago is $10.00 per hour.

So the per-flight compensation for each of the crew member is:

> One-Flight Compensation = Hourly Duty Pay * Flight Time + Per Diem * Layover Time (for non-home base location).

The formula to calculate the monthly total pay for each crew member is:

> Monthly Total Pay = Monthly Base Pay + Flight Compensations within This Month.

System architectural design

Air-X has selected Microsoft Dynamics CRM 2011 to implement their ACM system because of its flexibility and integration possibilities. The ACM system needs to integrate with an extranet portal to provide the compensation information to the flight crews. Here is a component diagram of the system:

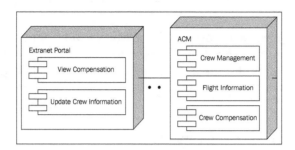

Defining the ACM data model

In the Airline Compensation Management system, we have identified the entities for the system: Airport, Flight Route, Flight, Crew Member, and Compensation.

- **Airport** is a custom entity that contains information related to the airport. Because the airport is in a specific location within the country, it also contains the "Per Diem" information, which we are going to use for the crew's compensation calculation.

- **Flight Route** is a custom entity containing the route template for a specific flight. It contains the flight number, departing and arriving locations planned departure time, and estimated flying time for the flight.

- **Flight** is a custom entity containing the actual flight information. It is an instance of the flight route. The Flight entity has the actual flight time and flight type information, which are used for the compensation calculation.

- **Crew Member** is going to leverage the out-of-the-box Contact entity to store personal information for a specific crew member. Crew can see and update their personal contact data from the company portal website. This entity also has the crew member's hourly pay rate and basic salary information, which is used for compensation calculation. The crew's compensation information is only accessible by the crew member and Air-X's management team.

- **Compensation** is a custom activity, which is new in CRM 2011. It contains the total payment for a completed flight that the crew member worked on. The total compensation for the flight is calculated automatically after the flight record is imported from the Aircrew system.

The next screenshot shows the entity relationships in ACM. An airport can have many flight routes. For each flight route, it has many of the same flights operating at different times. Each flight needs to compensate many crew members since there are many crew members serving the passengers on the plane.

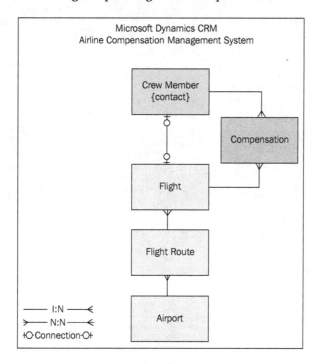

CRM 2011 customization improvement

The entity customization experience in CRM 2011 is similar to Microsoft Dynamics CRM 4.0, which allows you to customize almost all of the entities. However CRM 2011 has made some improvements to the overall customization experience. One of the improvements is that it allows a CRM user who has entity customization privileges to quickly bring up the form customization designer. All you have to do is click on the **Customize** tab within the entity record, as indicated in the following screenshot:

Additional customization improvements in CRM 2011 are that it allows you to create the attributes and relationships within the designer, it allows you to customize the left navigation items, and it also allows you to drag and drop the fields onto the form:

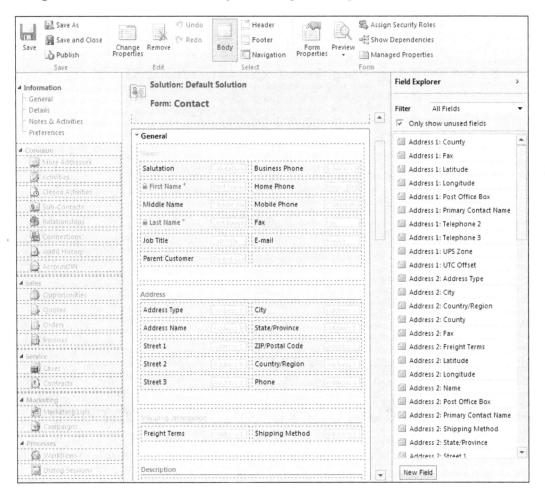

Entity

Creating entities in CRM 2011 offers an intuitive user-experience for system customizers. To create an entity, simply follow these steps:

1. Navigate to the ACM Solution.
2. Click **New** on the grid navigation menu.

3. Select **Entity** to bring up the entity form.

4. Fill in the information for your entity.

5. Click an **Save** and **Close**.

Form

In CRM 2011, each entity supports multiple interface forms. You can create multiple forms and mobile forms. This is different from CRM 4.0, which only supports a single form that can't be deleted. Each form in CRM 2011 ties to a specific security role. To create a new form, simply click on **New** on the form customization grid menu:

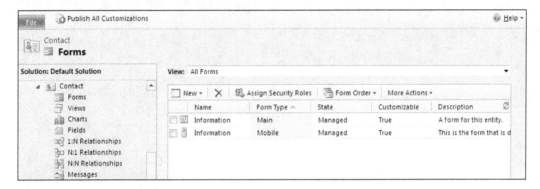

View

Views remain the same as in CRM 4.0. Views display data by using specified filters; these define how the data should be displayed in CRM.

Chart

Charts are new in CRM 2011. A chart presents the entity's data visually by mapping textual values on two axes: horizontal (x) and vertical (y).

Relationship

Relationships remain the same as in CRM 4.0. They still support one to many (1:N), many to one (N:1), and many to many (N:N) relationships. You can browse and set up relationships in the Solution Explorer.

Attribute

You may still use the old ways of creating the entity attribute by navigating to **Settings | Customizations | Customize System**. However, with the improvements to form customization, you can create attributes from within the form designer. Within the form designer, just click the **New Field** button in the Field Explorer to create your attribute. The following screenshots shows the attribute types in CRM 2011:

CRM 2011 has the following attribute types:

- Single Line of Text (nvarchar)
- Option Set (picklist or global picklist)
- Two Options (bit)
- Whole Number (int)
- Floating Point Number (float)
- Decimal Number (decimal)
- Currency (money)

- Multiple Lines of Text (ntext)
- Date and Time (datetime)
- Lookup (lookup)

Navigation

CRM 2011 has made it extremely easy to customize the left-hand navigation frame. It allows a CRM customizer to rename, remove, and reorder the navigation items within this frame.

To change the navigation group name, double-click on the group to bring up the Group properties window. Change the name of the group and then click on **OK** to save the change.

To remove the item link on the navigation, just select the item, and then click the **Remove** button on the ribbon.

Alternatively, you can control the item visibility by using user's security roles.

 You cannot remove a group (that is Sales, Service, and Marketing) from the Form Editor, but you can hide the group by removing all of items underneath it. In the following screenshot, the aforementioned three groups will be hidden on the form.

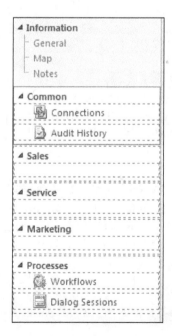

To rename a navigation item, double-click on the item to bring up the Relationship Properties window. Change the name in the **Label** textbox and then click on **OK** to save the change.

To re-order a navigation item, simply drag the item to the desired location; see the following screenshot:

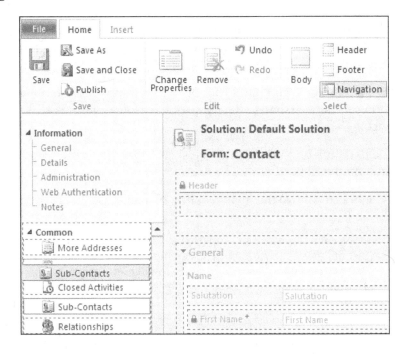

Header and Footer

Header and Footer are new in CRM 2011; you may put any of the same fields in the Header/Footer section as they are available in the Body section. All fields in the Header/Footer section are read-only on the form.

Configuring the ACM system

Now that we have an out-of-the-box development environment, let's first configure it. Because we use Microsoft Dynamics CRM 2011 as an xRM platform, we just focus on those settings that are used by our ACM system.

The term "xRM" stands for "Anything Relationship Management", and is used to refer to custom solutions that build on top of the Microsoft Dynamics CRM platform.

So Microsoft Dynamics CRM is not just managing the "customers"; it can be customized to manage "anything" that fits for the business requirement.

Administration

Navigate to **Settings** | **System** | **Administration**.

System settings

The **System Settings** module allows the configuration of global application settings such as general settings, calendar, formats, auditing, email, marketing, customization, Outlook, reporting, and goal settings. You can easily find and configure these in **System Settings**.

ACM has a requirement that:

- All usernames are set up with First Name and Last Name.
- Current Format is set to English: United States.
- Auditing is enabled for common entities.
- The tracking token prefix is set to: ACM.
- All other out-of-the-box settings are maintained.

Solution and publisher

Microsoft Dynamics CRM 2011 provides a rich framework on which the business application can be built. It has the notion of "solution" by providing full support to create, install, upgrade, and delete business applications that run on the CRM framework.

The solution concept is new to Microsoft Dynamics CRM 2011. A solution is a container of components designed to provide specific business functionality. The valid components that can be included in the solution are data model, modification to the CRM user interface, web resources such as images, HTML pages, JavaScript libraries, processes, plug-in code, and translations. Each solution has a publisher associated to it. A solution publisher represents the "author" who writes/provides this solution.

Solutions can be packaged as "managed" or as "unmanaged". All solutions are initially created as unmanaged solutions. When you create a "New" solution in CRM, this creates a container to hold references to the components in the system. Multiple unmanaged solutions can have references to the same component, however any changes performed on the component will be visible to all unmanaged solutions. Exporting any solution that contains the component will export all of the changes performed on the system. Importing an unmanaged solution always overwrites the components that it touches.

Managed solutions were designed for the final distribution of components. After initial development is done and the solution is ready to deploy to the production environment, you need to export it as managed. If a managed solution is imported into a different organization, the definition of the solution is locked and you may not add or remove any of the components within the solution. Managed solutions can be uninstalled and this will not affect your base system.

We will cover Solution and Publisher in detail later in *Chapter 10, Creating Eye Candy Effects with Particle Systems*.

In this project, we are going to create an unmanaged solution during our development. Once we complete the development, we will package it and export it as a managed solution for our production deployment.

Creating a solution publisher

To create a new publisher in CRM 2011, follow these steps:

1. Navigate to **Settings | Customizations | Publishers**.
2. Click on **New** to create a new publisher.
3. Populate the **Display Name** and **Prefix** fields by filling in the publisher form with the following information:

Display name	ACM publisher
Name:	acmpublisher
Prefix:	acm
Option Value Prefix:	10,000

The following screenshot shows the ACM Publisher form:

4. Click on **Save** and **Close**.

Creating a solution

To create a new solution in CRM 2011, follow these steps:

1. Navigate to **Settings | Solutions**.
2. Click on **New** to create a new solution.
3. Populate the **Display Name**, **Publisher**, and **Version** fields by filling in the solution form with the following information:

Display name	ACM solution
Name:	ACMSolution
Publisher:	ACM
Version:	1.0

The following screenshot shows the ACM Solution form:

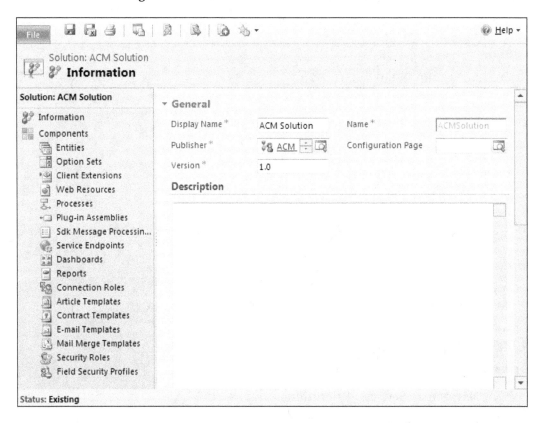

4. Click on **Save** and **Close**.

Creating an Entity for the ACM solution

Let's customize the ACM solution. Since we have created a solution for our project, the next step is to create the entities. In the ACM solution, we will have three custom entities (Airport, Flight Route, and Flight), one custom activity (Compensation), and one system entity (Crew Member [contact]).

So let's go ahead and create the custom entities first.

Go to **Settings | Solutions**, and double-click to open the ACM solution. In the solution components list, select the **Entities** node and then click on **New**. Fill in the Airport information, and then click the **Save** button on the toolbar:

Airport

The following table lists the entities that need to be defined, and their settings.

Entity	Customization
Definition	Entity Definition: • Display Name: Airport • Plural Name: Airports • Name: acm_airport • Ownership: Organization • Define as an activity entity: No • Display in Activity Menus: No • Description: Airport entity • Primary attribute: acm_name (Display Name: Airport Code) Areas that display this entity: • Workplace Options for Entity: • Notes (Includes attachments): Yes • Activities: Yes • Connections: Yes • Sending e-mail: No • Mail merge: No • Document management: No • Queues: No • Duplication detection: No • Auditing: No • Mobile Express: No • Reading pane in CRM for Outlook: No • Offline capability for CRM for Outlook: No
Forms	Main
Views	Active Airport (Default Public View) and other Views
Charts	-
Custom Relationships	1:N — Flight Route (custom label: Route From and Route To); Relationship Behavior: Referential

Note: Some options cannot be disabled after you enable them, so you can leave options unchecked if you are not sure about them during the entity creation.

Form customization

In the Airport entity, click on the **Forms** link in the left-hand navigation panel, and then double-click to open the Main form:

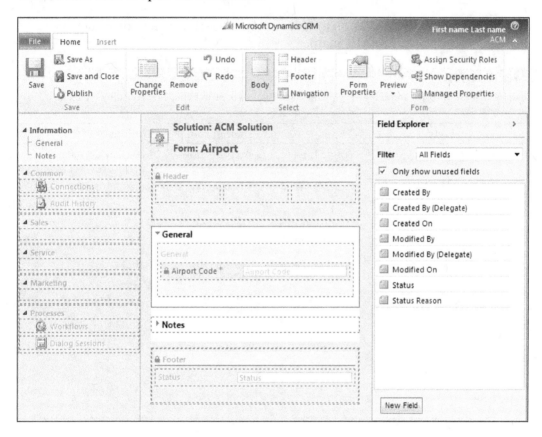

1. We need to change the field layout from two columns to one column: Double-click on the **Airport Code** field, go to the **Formatting** tab, select **One Column**, and then click **OK** to save the changes and go back to the Form Editor.

2. Next we need to insert some new fields (attribute) on the form: In CRM 2011, you can create attributes from the Form Editor: click the **Body** button on the ribbon, and the **Field Explorer** appears in the right-hand pane. You can create attributes by clicking the **New Field** button in the Explorer.

3. Follow the table to add new fields: Click the **New Field** button in the Field Explorer, and add **Airport Name**, **Time Zone**, **Country**, **City**, and **Per Diem**. After these fields have been created, drag them to the **General** tab on the Form Editor. And then click the **Save** button to save changes.

 Note: When adding an Option Set, if you want that option field to be used globally in the solution, you can select the **Existing Option Set** option and then click on **New** to create the **Option Set**.

Back in the Form Editor, click on the **Insert** tab on the ribbon, and then click on **IFRAME** (see below: IFRAME_map).

Main form

*All fields (except Notes and IFRAME) are Business Required, Searchable, and Auditing enabled.

	Field	Type	Description	Options
General	Airport Code	Single Line of Text	Airport code	Max length: 100
	Airport Name	Single Line of Text	Airport name	Max length: 100
	Time Zone	Whole Number (Time Zone)	Time zone	-
	Country	Single Line of Text	Country list (this is a demo list for the book)	**Label** **Value** United Kingdom 1 United States 2

Field	Type	Description	Options
City	Single Line of Text	Dependent picklist of 'Country' (this is a demo list for the book)	**Label** **Value** London (UK) 1 Birmingham (UK) 2 Washington D.C (US)) 3 Seattle (US) 4 New York (US) 5
Per Diem	Currency	Hourly payment of this location	Min: 0 Max: 100 Precision: Currency Precision
Notes	Note Text	Notes	-	-

Now that we have created the Airport main form, click the **Preview** button on the ribbon and select **Create Form**, which will show us what the form looks like.

Click the **Save** and **Close** button on the ribbon to go back to the solution panel.

View customization

In the Airport entity, click on **Views** to open the view list; double-click on the Active Airport view, to open it. Click on the **Created On** column and click the **Remove** button on the right-hand Common Task panel to remove this column. Click on **Add Columns** to add Airport Name, Country, and City columns to the View. Double-click on the column to change the Width for each column. Use the **Left** and **Right** buttons to change the column placement.

Views—Active Airports and other Views

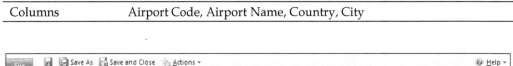

Columns	Airport Code, Airport Name, Country, City

Now you know how to create and customize entities, attributes, views, relationships, and navigations. Do the same for the remaining entities for the project.

Flight route

Entity	Customization
Information	Entity Definition: • Display Name: Flight Route • Plural Name: Flight Routes • Name: acm_flightroute • Ownership: Organization • Define as an activity entity: No • Display in Activity Menus: No • Description: Flight Route entity • Primary attribute: acm_name (Display Name: Flight Route) Areas that display this entity: • Workplace Options for Entity: • Notes (Includes attachments): Yes • Activities: Yes • Connections: Yes • Sending e-mail: No • Mail merge: No • Document management: No • Queues: No • Duplication detection: No • Auditing: No • Mobile Express: No • Reading pane in CRM for Outlook: No • Offline capability for CRM for Outlook: No
Forms	Main
Views	Active Flight Routes (Default Public View) and other Views
Charts	-

Entity	Customization
Custom Relationships	1:N – Flight; Relationship Behavior: Referential
	N:1 – Airport; Relationship Behavior: Referential

Main form

*All fields (except Notes) are Business Required, Searchable, and Auditing enabled.

	Field	Type	Description	Options
General	Flight Route	Single Line of Text	Name of the flight route	Max length: 100
	From	Lookup	Unique identifier of the departure airport code	-
	To	Lookup	Unique identifier of the arrival airport code	-
	Miles	Whole Number (None)	Miles between departure and arrival airport	Min: 0 Max: 100000
Notes	Note Text	Notes	-	-

Relationships

Like CRM 4.0, you can create entity relationships (1:N, N:1, N:N) from the Entity Editor. Alternatively, in CRM 2011 you can also create an N:1 relationship directly from the From Editor by clicking the **New Field** button, then selecting **Lookup type**.

Because we will create two N:1 relationships from the Flight Route entity to the Airport entity, there will be two relationship links in the left-hand navigation panel of the Airport entity, and they will both call: Flight Route. So in this case, we need to change the name to make it different: go to the **Airport** entity | **1:N Relationships**, and then open the Flight relationships (Primary Entity = Airport, Related Entity = Flight Route), change the Display Option to "Use Custom Label", Custom Label: "Route From" (and for the other one, where Name is "acm_acm_airport_acm_ flightroute_to", change the custom label to: Route To). You may also change the Relationship Behavior here.

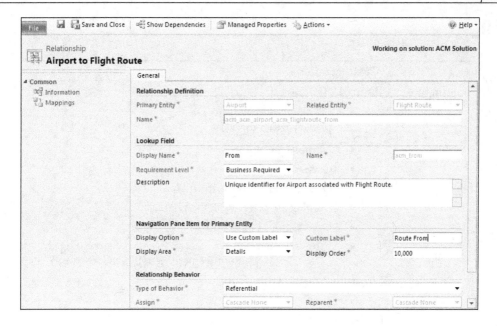

Views—Active Flight Routes and other Views

Columns	Flight Route, From, To, Miles

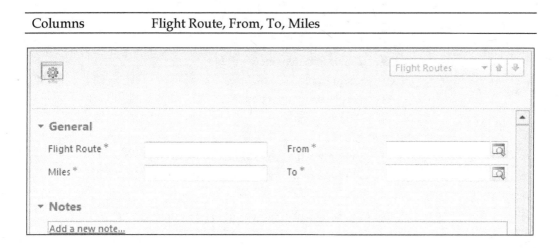

Flight

Entity	Customization
Information	Entity Definition:
	• Display Name: Flight
	• Plural Name: Flights
	• Name: acm_flight
	• Ownership: Organization
	• Define as an activity entity: No
	• Display in Activity Menus: No
	• Description: Flight entity
	• Primary attribute: acm_name (Display Name: Flight; Requirement Level: No Constraint)
	Areas that display this entity:
	• Workplace
	Options for Entity:
	• Notes (Includes attachments): Yes
	• Activities: Yes
	• Connections: Yes
	• Sending e-mail: No
	• Mail merge: No
	• Document management: No
	• Queues: No
	• Duplication detection: No
	• Auditing: No
	• Mobile Express: No
	• Reading pane in CRM for Outlook: No
	• Offline capability for CRM for Outlook: No
Forms	Main
Views	Active Flights (Default Public View) and other Views
Charts	-
Custom Relationships	1:N — Compensation; Relationship Behavior: Referential
	N:1 — Flight Route; Relationship Behavior: Referential

Main form

*All fields (except Flight and Notes) are Business Required, Searchable, and Auditing enabled.

	Field	Type	Description	Options
General	Flight Name	Single Line of Text	This filed is populated by workflow. Requirement Level: No Constraint. Layout: 3columns. Display: In the header of main form.	Max length: 100
	Flight Route	Lookup	Unique identifier of the of the flight route	Flight is an instance of a Flight Route
	Departure Time	Date and Time	Local departure date and time	Format: Date and Time
	Arrival Time	Date and Time	Local arrival date and time	Format: Date and Time
	Flight Time	Whole Number (Duration)	In flight hours	-
	Layover Time	Whole Number (Duration)	Off flight hours of the destination	-
	Flight Type	Options Set	The Red Eye/ Holiday/Polar line flights will double the hourly payment. (Default value: Normal)	**Label** **Value** Normal Flight 1 Red-Eye Flight 2 Holiday Flight 3 Polar Flight 4

	Field	Type	Description	Options
Flight Crew	CrewConnection	Sub-Grid	Insert a new tab called "tab_crew" on the form; and then insert a Sub-Grid inside the tab	Sub-Grid properties: • Records: Only Related Records • Entity: Connections (Connected From) • Default View: Active Connections
Notes	Note Text	Notes	-	-

Form header

The Flight (name) will be generated by Workflow, so Flight Name = Flight Route + Departure Time.

So we can put the Flight (name) in the form header. On the Form Editor, click **Header** on the ribbon, then drag the **Flight** field onto the **Header** section, and then increase the width by three columns.

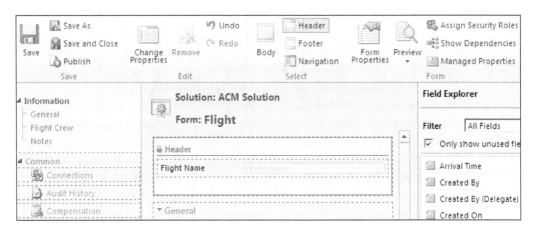

Double-click on the Flight field in the Body section, deselect the **Visible by default** option to make sure that the Flight field only appears in the Header.

Views—Active Flights and other Views

Columns	Flight, Flight Route, Departure Time, Arrival Time, Created On

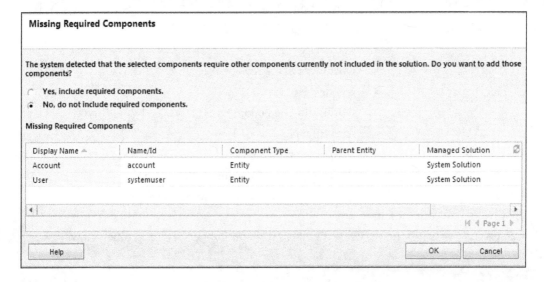

Now that we have created three custom entities, for Crew Members, we will use the system entity: contact. So go to the **ACM Solution Components** list, click on **Entities**, and then click on **Add Existing | Contact**. Select **No, do not include required components**, because we don't need those entities in the ACM solution:

When you click on the Contact entity in the ACM Solution Components, you may notice that some options are grayed out, so just leave this as it is. Some of these can be changed in SiteMap.

Crew Member

Entity	Customization
Information	Entity Definition:
	• Display Name: Crew Member
	• Plural Name: Crew Members
	• Name: contact
	• Ownership: User or Team
	• Define as an activity entity: No
	• Display in Activity Menus: No
	• Description: Crew Member entity
	• Primary attribute: fullname (Display Name: Full Name)
	Areas that display this entity:
	• (Default Settings)
	Options for Entity:
	• Notes (Includes attachments): Yes
	• Activities: Yes
	• Connections: Yes
	• Sending e-mail: Yes
	• Mail merge: Yes
	• Document management: No
	• Queues: No
	• Duplication detection: Yes
	• Auditing: No
	• Mobile Express: No
	• Reading pane in CRM for Outlook: No
	• Offline capability for CRM for Outlook: Yes
Forms	Main
Views	Active Crew Members (Default Public View) and other Views
Charts	-

Entity	Customization
Custom Relationships	1:N - Compensation; Relationship Behavior: Referential

Main form

*Monthly Base Pay and Hourly Duty Pay are custom fields that are Business Required, Searchable, and Auditing enabled. All other fields are system default fields—we try to keep it really simple in this book, although in reality there will be more fields for this entity.

	Field	Type	Description	Options
General	Salutation	Single Line of Text	CRM default field	Max length: 50
	First Name	Single Line of Text	CRM default field	Max length: 100
	Middle Name	Single Line of Text	CRM default field	Max length: 100
	Last Name	Single Line of Text	CRM default field	Max length: 50
	Employee ID	Single Line of Text	CRM default field (Employee)	Max length: 50
	Business Phone	Single Line of Text	CRM default field	Max length: 50
	Mobile Phone	Single Line of Text	CRM default field	Max length: 50
	E-mail	E-mail	CRM default field	Max length: 100
	Address			
	Address Name	Single Line of Text	CRM default field	Max length: 200
	Street 1	Single Line of Text	CRM default field	Max length: 50
	Street 2	Single Line of Text	CRM default field	Max length: 50
	Street 3	Single Line of Text	CRM default field	Max length: 50
	City	Single Line of Text	CRM default field	Max length: 50
	Province	Single Line of Text	CRM default field	Max length: 50

Field	Type	Description	Options
Postal Code	Single Line of Text	CRM default field	Max length: 20
Country	Single Line of Text	CRM default field	Max length: 50

Detail		Professional Information		

	Field	Type	Description	Options
	Department	Single Line of Text	CRM default field	Max length: 100
	Job Title	Single Line of Text	CRM default field	Max length: 100
	Monthly Base Pay	Currency	Monthly base pay	Min: 0
			(This field enables Field Security)	Max: 100,000
				Precision: Currency Precision
	Hourly Duty Pay	Currency	Hourly duty pay of the crew member	Min: 0
				Max: 100
			(This field enables Field Security)	Precision: Currency Precision
Owner	Owner	Unique identifier of the user or team who owns the record.	CRM default field	Unselect the "Visible by default" option
	Description	Multiple lines of Text	CRM default field	Max: 2000
Notes	Note Text	Notes	-	-

Entity navigation pane

The out-of-the-box Contact entity has some default links in the entity navigation pane; we can remove these links from the entity's Form Editor:

1. Under the Common node, only keep Activities, Closed Activities, Connections, Audit History, and Compensation.

2. Remove everything under Sales, Service, and Marketing nodes.

3. Keep the Processes node and sub items.

Views—Active Flight Attendants and other Views

Columns	Full Name, Department, Job Title, Business Phone

 Note: Because we renamed the system entity "Contact" to "Crew Member", we need to rename it for all related Fields, Views, and Messages that contain the word "Contact". We also need to rename it in the Relationships text and the Help document if necessary.

You cannot delete System Views in a Managed solution, but you may deactivate the View by selecting **View | More Actions | Deactivate**.

The last major entity we will use in this book is a custom activity (new introduced in CRM 2011) entity called Compensation. Each flight will generate a compensation record for each crew member who works on this flight.

 Note: When you create a custom activity, some options are pre-configured.

Compensation

Entity	Customization
Information	Entity Definition: • Display Name: Compensation • Plural Name: Compensations • Name: acm_compensation • Primary attribute: subject (Subject) • Ownership: User or Team • Define as an activity entity: Yes • Display in Activity Menus: Yes • Description: Compensation entity Options for Entity: • Notes (Includes attachments): Yes • Activities: No • Connections: Yes • Sending e-mail: No • Mail merge: No • Document management: No • Queues: Yes • Duplication detection: No • Auditing: No • Mobile Express: No • Reading pane in CRM for Outlook: No • Offline capability for CRM for Outlook: Yes
Forms	Main
Views	All Compensations (Default Public View) and other Views
Charts	-
Custom Relationships	1:N — Compensation; Relationship Behavior: Referential N:1 — Flight Route; Relationship Behavior: Referential

Main form

*All fields in the General tab are Business Required, Searchable, and Auditing enabled.

	Field	Type	Description	Options
Header	Compensation	Currency	One-Flight Compensation for the crew member (This field enables Field Security)	Min: 0 Max: 10,000 Precision: Currency Precision
General	Subject	Text	The subject of the compensation	Max length: 100
	Flight	Lookup	Unique identifier of the of the flight	Flight is an instance of a Flight Route
	Crew Member	Lookup	Unique identifier of the crew member	-
	Owner	Owner	Unique identifier of the user or team who owns the record.	Unselect the "Visible by default" option
Detail	Layover Time	Whole Number (Duration)	Same field of the Flight entity	Read-Only
	Flight Type	Options Set	Same field of the Flight entity	Read-Only
Notes	Note Text	Notes	-	-

Views—All Compensations and other Views

Columns	Subject, Crew Member, Flight, Date Created

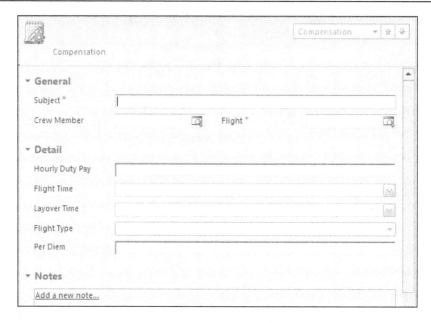

Publishing customizations

Now that we have performed the initial user interface customizations, we need to publish our customizations for them to be visible to CRM users. You can publish all customizations at one time, or publish them individually. See the following screenshot:

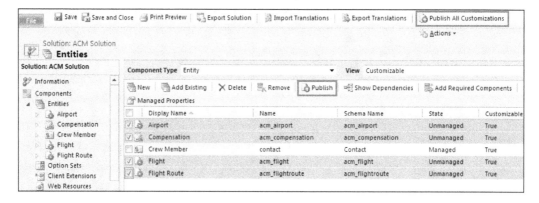

ACM system security structure

Microsoft Dynamics CRM 2011 security is handled by security roles similar to CRM 4.0. You can create a security role for a specific group of people. In our ACM system we can draw a security role decision tree based on the requirement:

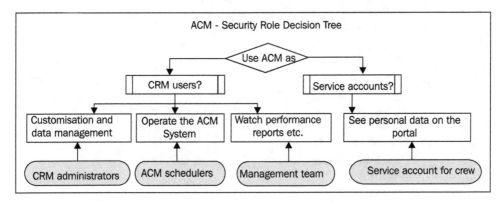

We have four security roles identified for the ACM system, namely:

1. **CRM Administrator Role**: This role has full access to the system. These are the people who maintain the system.

2. **ACM Schedulers Role**: This role has permission to access the system to view and update certain information regarding flights. It doesn't have permissions to delete records or customize the system.

3. **ACM Manager Role**: This role has permission to access all data within the ACM system. It doesn't have permission to customize the system.

4. **Flight Crew Role**: This role only has access to see data at the personal level. It doesn't have access to data at a higher level.

For the CRM Administrator Role, we can leverage the default "System Administrator" role. We will walk you through the process of creating a new security role in CRM 2011:

- Navigate to the Security Administration area by going to **Settings | Administration | Security Role**.

- Select the **System Administrator** security role.

- Click **More Actions** from the grid menu, and then select **Copy Role**:

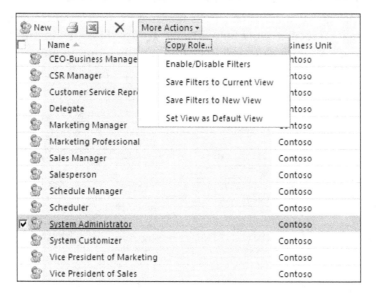

- In the **Copy Role** dialog form, enter **ACM Scheduler** in the **New Role Name** textbox.

- Click on **OK** to copy the security role.

- Once the security role has been successfully copied, configure the security role by following the instructions indicated in the following table:

Core Records	Marketing	Sales	Service	Customization
Clear all privileges on the following entities: Account, Customer Relationship, Lead, Opportunity, Opportunity Relationship, Relationship Role, and Subject", by clicking on the corresponding row name. Clear the "Delete" privilege on all entities.	Clear all privileges on all entities by clicking on the corresponding row or column name.			Clear all "Create", "Write", and "Delete" privileges on all entities by clicking on the corresponding column name.

Summary

That's it! In this chapter, we have identified the Airline Compensation Management System that we are going to build in this book. You were also introduced to some of the new and improved features in CRM customization. Throughout this book, we are going to show you all of the new features of Microsoft Dynamic CRM 2011 by building this system.

3
Data Import

Microsoft Dynamics CRM 2011 and Microsoft Dynamics CRM Online both provide an out-of-the-box Import Data Wizard tool, as well as the Import file/data web service which provides additional capabilities that are not available in the Import Data Wizard.

There are also other options when considering Data Import / Migration to Microsoft Dynamics CRM, such as using third-party tools such as Scribe Insight or C360 Import Manager. The choice is based on the project.

In this task, we will populate some sample data for testing and further development into CRM by using the new Import Data Wizard.

CRM 2011 Import Data Wizard

The Import Data Wizard has been enhanced in Microsoft Dynamics CRM 2011. It takes some of the functionality from the CRM 4.0 DMM (Data Migration Manager), as well as adding some new features. We will walk through the new Import Data Wizard along with our ACM system.

Initially we need to populate three entity records into CRM: Crew Members, Airports, and Flight Routes. We will import Crew Member records with notes and attachments. Airport and Flight Route are connected entities, so we are going to import both entity records together (in a single CSV file) using the Import Data Wizard.

Supported file types

The Import Data Wizard supports XML Spreadsheets (`.xml`), Simple Text (`.csv` or `.txt`), and multiple files (`.zip`). By default, the maximum size of a file is 8 MB, which means:

- Any `.csv`, `.txt`, or `.xml` file must not exceed 8 MB

- Any individual file inside the `.zip` file must not exceed 8 MB and the total size of the `.zip` file, including the attachment folder, must not exceed 32 MB

> There is a work around to change the default size limitation; see: `http://billoncrmtech.blogspot.com/2008/07/data-import-wizard-will-not-upload.html`.

Single entity import with an attachment

First of all, we are going to import the first entity: Crew Member. For each Crew Member record, we also need to import a photo as an attachment.

Downloading a template for the import

Microsoft Dynamics CRM 2011 provides the Data Import Template for entities. The template is in XML Spreadsheet 2003 format, with an `.xml` extension. You can download it by going to **Settings | Data Management | Templates for Data Import**. Alternatively, to download the Data Import Template for Crew Members, go to **ACM homepage | Crew Members entity**. On the ribbon bar you will see a button called **Import Data**. Click on the text **Import Data** below the button, and then click **Download Template for Import**:

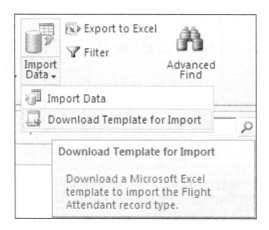

Open the XML file using Microsoft Excel; you will see that each column corresponds to a field on the Crew Member main form. It also indicates (via bolded column text) all mandatory fields for the record.

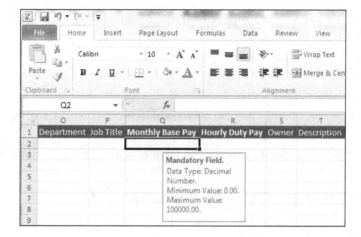

You may notice that all mandatory fields are bold text. So make sure that these fields have valid data for importing.

You also see a unique identifier data type (lookup) on the Spreadsheet call: Owner.

Owner is a system mandatory field that appears in all user-owned entities. The owner data can be populated by the data import process—we don't need to fill in this field—so remove the Owner column.

Filling in the template

The next screenshot shows the basic information for Crew Member. Save it to XML Spreadsheet 2003 format, and name it Crew Member.xml.

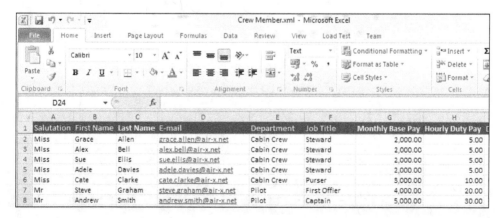

There is something we should know about the template:

- The workbook contains a field format. Users should follow this format when filling in data.

- The workbook contains a picklist value for Picklist format fields, which is handy for users when filling in data.

- For the Lookup data type, the value should match the primary field of the lookup entity. That is, in our case, the team value **Cabin Crew** and **Pilot** are exactly matching the team names we entered in ACM, earlier.

- Do not use non-printable characters, such as newline (\n) or return (\r) characters.

- The workbook format must be compatible with XML Spreadsheet 2003.

Including a note and an attachment

As we mentioned, we are going to import a photo as an attachment for each Crew Member, in one data import process.

Attachment, in Microsoft Dynamics CRM 2011 is mapped to the Note entity which has a relationship to the related parent entity (Crew Member). In order to import both entities in parallel, we need to create a separate XML Spreadsheet 2003 workbook for Note.

 Note: Make sure the entity that you are importing has Notes associated with it. You can check it from entity options.

The next screenshot shows the basic information for an Attachment (Note); save it to XML Spreadsheet 2003 format, and name it Note.xml.

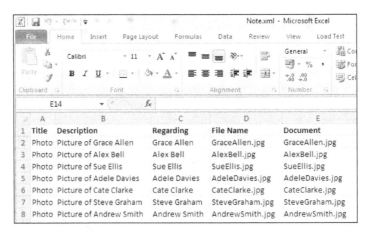

In this demo, all crew members have different names, so we can import Crew Member and Notes together using the Automatic Mapping option in CRM 2011.

- The **Regarding** column will look up the primary field of the related entity; in our case it is `contact.fullname`.

- **File Name** is the attachment name. It tells the data import process which attachment to upload; all attachments should be put in a separate folder called **Attachments**. See the next screenshot for an example.

- **Document** is the attachment name after loading it into CRM. It must have a unique name across the workbook.

The next step is to create a folder called `Attachments`, put all of the pictures into that folder, zip it along with `Crew Member.xml` and `Note.xml`, and call it `Crew Members.zip`. Note that the zip file can contain either CSV files or XML Spreadsheet 2003 files, but not both. See the next screenshot as an example:

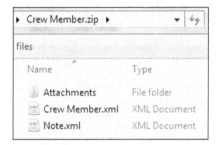

Duplicate data detection

Microsoft Dynamics CRM 2011 has an out-of-the-box duplicate data detection function, which provides the capability to detect and handle duplicate data. To avoid importing duplicate data into the ACM system, we need to take a look at the duplicate detection settings: Go to the **ACM homepage| Data Management | Duplicate Detection Settings**.

Make sure that the **Enable duplicate detection** option is enabled and that the **During data import** option is selected. Then click on **OK** to save your changes and return to the previous screen.

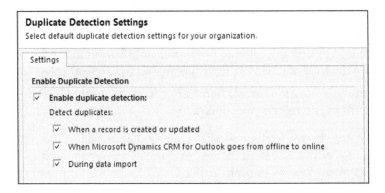

Now we need to create a rule that tells the system how to identify a duplicated record. Double-click to open the **Duplicate Detection Rules**; we can see that there are four rules out-of-the-box. Because none of these will be used in our system we can select all and then delete them.

Click the **New** button to set up the rule as shown below, save it, and then click the **Publish** button to activate the rule.

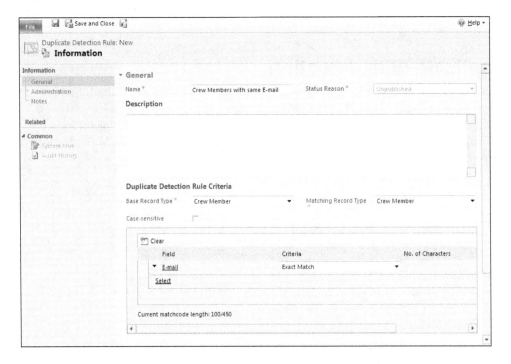

The above rule tells the system if an importing Crew Member has the same **E-mail** as any existing Crew Member in the system. This is a duplicated record and therefore should not be imported. CRM prompts users before saving or importing potential duplicate records:

- If you don't see the entity name in the Base/Matching Record Type list, then you might need to enable the "Duplicate detection" of that entity.
- All conditions implicitly have an "AND" connector. That is, if you set up a rule with two conditions: "E-mail exact match, Last Name exact match", the system will only identify a duplicate record when this record's E-mail and Last Name exactly match an existing record which has the same values.
- You can create a separate rule if you want to use the "OR" connector.
- All conditions for one rule are combined into a matchcode. (A matchcode is a code created for every record to which a duplicate-detection rule might apply, and is used as part of the process for detecting duplicates. The matchcodes for new and updated records are created every five minutes, rather than when a record is created. A matchcode has a maximum length limit of 450 characters.)

By default, duplicate detection is available when a record is created or updated. This includes when a record created with the Microsoft Dynamics CRM for Outlook is tracked.

Duplicate Detection has some limitations that we should be aware of:

- If you enter a duplicate record within a few minutes of entering the first record, CRM will not detect the duplicate record because the matchcode is only created every five minutes for new and updated records.
- After publishing a duplicate detection rule, increasing the length of fields that are included in the duplicate detection criteria could exceed the matchcode length limit. This could result in duplicates not being detected.
- Duplicates cannot be detected when a user merges records, converts a lead, or saves an activity as completed.
- By default, duplicates are not detected during synchronization—that is, when the Microsoft Dynamics CRM for Outlook goes from offline to online.
- Each time you define an import, the choice of checking for duplicates is available. So it is possible to create duplicate records during data import.

To work around the above limitations, we may schedule Duplicate Detection Jobs. (A job that runs in the background; you can request e-mail notification when the job completes, with a link to the page where it can be resolved.) To schedule a **Duplicate Detection Job**, go to **ACM Settings | Duplicate Detection**. It's very straight forward, and you can try it yourself.

Data import using ZIP file

Go to **ACM Workplace | Crew Member** and click the **Import Data** button to start the **Import Data Wizard**. Browse to select the Crew Members.zip file, and then click **Next**. The Wizard will find two files in the ZIP file; click **Next**.

Select the **Default (Automatic Mapping)** option, and then click **Next**.

Because the columns are exactly mapped to the field Display Name, this saves our time to map it manually. You will see that both **Crew Member** and **Note** are successfully mapped to the target record types:

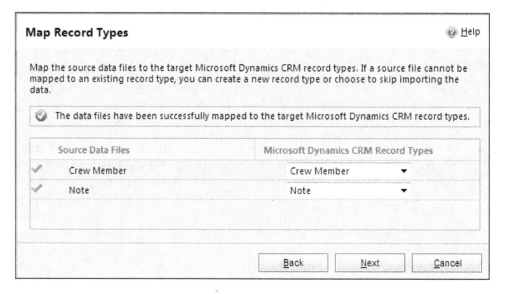

Click **Next** again. This will bring us to the **Review Settings and Import Data** screen. Select **No** on **Allow Duplicates**, select an owner for the imported records, and then click the **Submit** button:

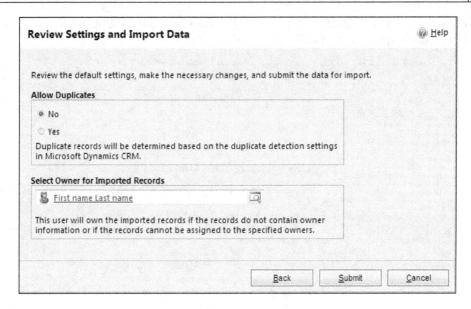

Now the data has been successfully submitted for Import, and we will see a "Congratulations!" message. However this just indicates that the data has been submitted for import; that doesn't mean the import has succeeded. It's just half way finished. The system will parse the import file, then transform the parsed data, and finally it will upload the transformed data to the target Microsoft Dynamics CRM server. Fortunately, these processes (parse-transform-upload) are done by the asynchronous jobs that run in the background.

To know whether everything has been successfully imported, click the **Imports** link:

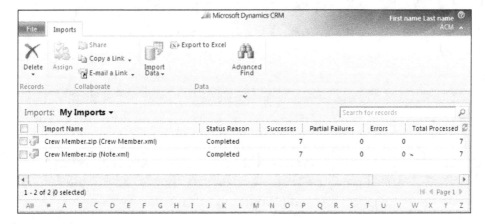

If you open an **Import Source File**, you will see what has been imported, what has been partially imported, and a list of the failures:

To remove the imported data, select the import source file, and click the drop-down icon for the **Delete** button on the ribbon. Here we can see three options, which are all intuitive and meaningful.

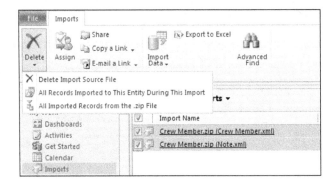

Importing multiple entities with Data Map

We have imported some Crew Member sample data, and are next going to import some Airport and Flight Route sample data.

In Microsoft Dynamics CRM 2011, you can import data from one source file or from several source files. A source file can contain data for one entity type or for multiple entity types.

Data Map

The Import Data Tool doesn't know that we want to create two types of records by using a single CSV file unless we provide a Data Map (a file that contains information about how data from a source system corresponds to data in Microsoft Dynamics CRM) for it.

You can create a Data Map by using any XML editing tool. As a starting point, we want to see what a Data Map looks like, and will work from there. Go to **ACM Settings | Data Management | Data Maps**. Select **Active Data Maps** for the view, then select **For Generic Map for Contact and Account**, and click the **Export** button on the toolbar.

Use Microsoft XML Notepad 2007 to open the Data Map XML file. It looks like this:

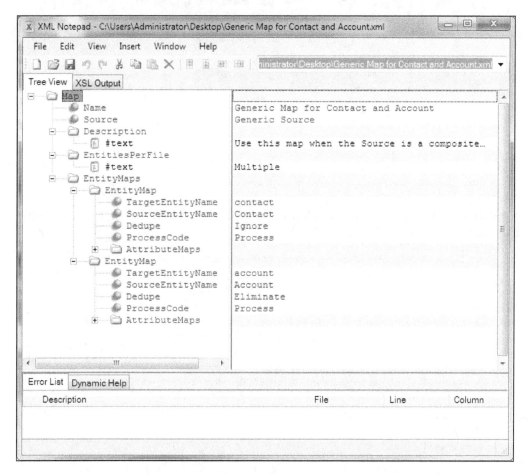

As we can see here, this Data Map is being used for Account/Contact data import. Now we need to update and simplify it so that the Data Map can be used for Airport/Flight Route data import:

1. Update the **TargetEntityName** and the **SourceEntityName**.

2. Change **Dedupe** from **Ignore** to **Eliminate**. This makes sure that we don't import duplicate records.

3. Delete the **Description** folder and the two **AttributeMaps** subfolders.

The following screenshot shows the final result:

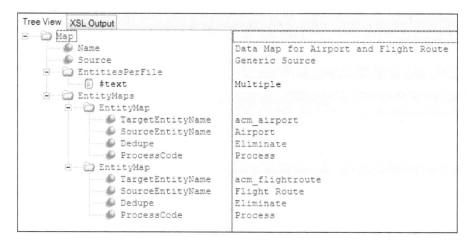

Now that we have a minimal Data Map for Airport and Flight Route, the XML looks like this:

```
<Map Name="Data Map for Airport and Flight Route"
     Source="Generic Source">
<EntitiesPerFile>Multiple</EntitiesPerFile>
<EntityMaps>
  <EntityMap TargetEntityName="acm_airport"
    SourceEntityName="Airport" Dedupe="Eliminate"
    ProcessCode="Process"/>
  <EntityMap TargetEntityName="acm_flightroute"
    SourceEntityName="Flight Route" Dedupe="Eliminate"
    ProcessCode="Process"/>
</EntityMaps>
</Map>
```

Save the data map file. Click the **Import** button on the Data Maps toolbar, upload the Data Map to CRM, and activate it. See the following screenshot for Data Maps:

A single CSV file

Air-X provides a single CSV file that contains both Airport and Flight Route information. Our task is to import it into CRM and create two types of entity records: Airport and Flight Route. We may split them and then import them separately. However, in Microsoft Dynamics CRM 2011 you can import multiple entities using a single data source, with Data Map.

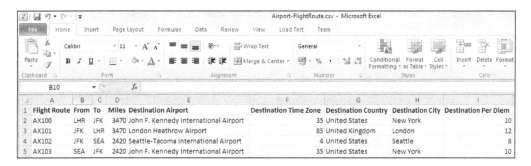

 The TimeZone has been replaced with the TimeZone code in this source file, in order for CRM to understand it during the data import. You can find the TimeZone code values by using IE Developer Toolbar.

```
<select name="acm_timezone" tabIndex="1070" class="ms-crm-SelectBox " id="acm_timezone" styl
  <option title="" value=""/>
  <option title="(GMT) Casablanca" value="84">
  <option title="(GMT) Coordinated Universal Time" value="92">
  <option title="(GMT) Greenwich Mean Time : Dublin, Edinburgh, Lisbon, London" value="85">
  <option title="(GMT) Monrovia, Reykjavik" value="99">
```

Export the Excel Spreadsheet to a CSV (comma delimited) (*.csv) file and then open it via Notepad, just to make sure you know what the delimiter is.

- You need to make sure that none of the fields in Excel Spreadsheet contain the delimiter. If one has, try using a different delimiter, or replace/remove the delimiter in the field value.

- When exporting to a CSV file, you can choose the delimiter by going to the Computer's **Control Panel** | **Region and Language** | **Additional settings**, then change the "List separator". The CRM Import Data Wizard only supports four types of field delimiter:

  1. Comma (,).
  2. Colon (:).
  3. Semicolon (;).
  4. Tab character (\t).

Data import using Data Map

Click the **Import Data** button on the ribbon, and then navigate to the CSV file that we created with both Airport and Flight Route information.

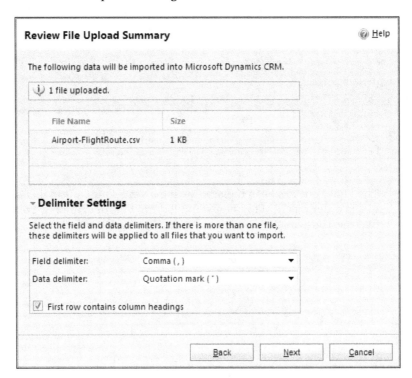

Make sure that you choose the correct Field delimiter and Data delimiter for the import file.

Select the customized map that we just created: "Data Map for Airport and Flight Route", and then click **Next**.

Because we didn't set the attribute maps in our XML file, we can do it here:

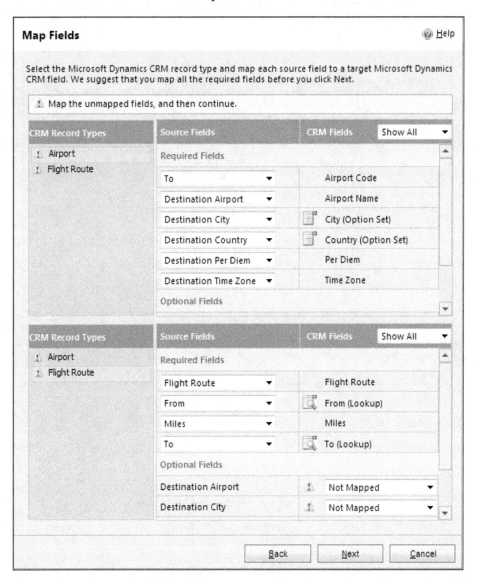

At this stage, we can save this data map for future imports, so that we don't have to map the attributes again.

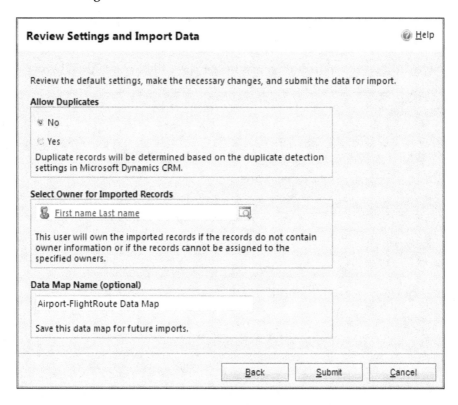

Submit this, and after a while both the Airport records and the Flight Route records are created in CRM:

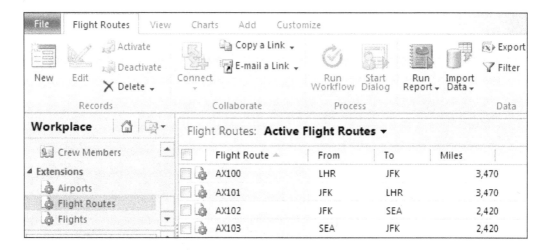

Data update

General speaking, the Import Data Wizard doesn't support data update, so each time the Import Data Wizard will create new records in CRM.

 Using Import Data Wizard, we can update user records if user exist in CRM—this is an exception.

A simple way to update CRM data is: export them using the XML Spreadsheet 2003 format, and then update using Excel, then import the XML into CRM.

You can use the Advanced Find function to select records you want to edit, then click on the Export Data to Excel button on the toolbar, the following dialog box will pop up. Select the Static worksheet with records from this page option and check Make this data available for re-importing by including required column headings. Next time when you import using this XML file, the corresponding data in CRM will be updated:

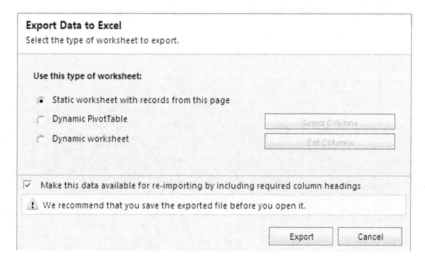

You might have noticed that there is a limitation of the ..records from this page, so if you have lots of data that you want to export and import, this method isn't an ideal solution.

Following example of how to programmatically insert/udpate (if data exist) Flight Routes with a CSV file.

More detail about the Microsoft Dynamics CRM 2011 server-side programming will be introduced in *Chpater 5, Server-Side Programming*.

```
/*
 * Update Flight Route if it exists in CRM; Otherwise Insert. *
 *
 * FlightRoutes.csv
 * Name;From;To;Miles
 * FR001;JFK;LHR;20000
 * FR002;JFK;SEA;30000
 *
 * */

using System;
using System.Collections.Generic;
using System.Linq;
using System.Text;
using System.ServiceModel.Description;
using System.Net;
using System.IO;
using Microsoft.Xrm.Sdk.Client;
using Microsoft.Xrm.Sdk;

namespace InsertUpdateFlightRoute
{
  class Program
  {
    static void Main(string[] args)
    {
      Uri OrganizationUri = new
                       Uri("http://bps:5555/ACM/XRMServices/
                       2011/Organization.svc");
      Uri HomeRealmUri = null;
      ClientCredentials Credentials = new ClientCredentials();
      Credentials.Windows.ClientCredential =
                       CredentialCache.DefaultNetworkCredentials;

      try
      {
        //Initializes a new instance of the CRM
          OrganizationServiceProxy class.
        using (OrganizationServiceProxy serviceProxy = new
```

```
                    OrganizationServiceProxy(OrganizationUri,
                    HomeRealmUri, Credentials, null))
{
    serviceProxy.EnableProxyTypes();
    IOrganizationService service =
                            (IOrganizationService)serviceProxy;

    //Read the csv file into the routes array.
    var routes =
                    File.ReadAllLines("FlightRoutes.csv").
                    Skip(1).Select(line =>
    {
        //Split columns by ;
        string[] fields = line.Split(";".ToCharArray());
        return new
        {
            fRoute = fields[0],
            fFrom = fields[1],
            fTo = fields[2],
            fMiles = fields[3]
        };

    }).ToArray();

    foreach (var route in routes)
    {
        //Query record in CRM: update the record if exist; insert
          the record if doesnot exist.
        acm_flightroute fr = getRoute(service, route.fRoute);

        if (fr != null)
        {
            //Record exist - update the Flight Route.
            fr.acm_name = route.fRoute;
            fr.acm_From = new
                    EntityReference(acm_airport.EntityLogicalName,
                    getAirport(service, route.fFrom));
            fr.acm_To = new
                    EntityReference(acm_airport.EntityLogicalName,
                    getAirport(service, route.fTo));
            fr.acm_Miles = int.Parse(route.fMiles);

            fr.EntityState = EntityState.Changed;

            try
```

```
                {
                  serviceProxy.Update(fr);
                }
                catch (Exception ex)
                {
                  errorHandler(ex);
                  continue;
                }
              }
              else
              {
                //Record doesnot exist - insert the Flight Route.
                acm_flightroute newFlightRoute = new acm_flightroute()
                {
                  acm_name = route.fRoute,
                  acm_Miles = int.Parse(route.fMiles),
                  acm_From = new
                          EntityReference(acm_airport.EntityLogicalName,
                          getAirport(service, route.fFrom)),
                  acm_To = new
                          EntityReference(acm_airport.EntityLogicalName,
                          getAirport(service, route.fTo))
                };
                try
                {
                  serviceProxy.Create(newFlightRoute);
                }
                catch (Exception ex)
                {
                  errorHandler(ex);
                  continue;
                }
              }
            }
          }
        }
      }
      catch (Exception ex)
      {
        errorHandler(ex);
      }

      Console.ReadLine();
    }

    //Display Errors.
```

```csharp
private static void errorHandler(Exception ex)
{
  Console.WriteLine(ex.Message + ex.InnerException);
  //Console.ReadLine();
}


//Return the Airport ID.
private static Guid getAirport(IOrganizationService service,
                              string airportcode)
{
  using (OrganizationServiceContext orgContext = new
        OrganizationServiceContext(service))
  {
    var query = from a in orgContext.CreateQuery<acm_airport>()
          where a.acm_name.Equals(airportcode)
          select a;
    if (query.FirstOrDefault() != null)
      return query.FirstOrDefault().acm_airportId.Value;
    else
      return Guid.Empty;
  }
}


//Return the Flight Route.
private static acm_flightroute getRoute(IOrganizationService
                                service, string routename)
{
  using (OrganizationServiceContext orgContext = new
        OrganizationServiceContext(service))
  {
    var query = from r in
                  orgContext.CreateQuery<acm_flightroute>()
          where r.acm_name.Equals(routename)
          select r;

    if (query.FirstOrDefault() != null)
      return query.FirstOrDefault();
    else
      return null;
  }
 }
 }
}
```

CRM data import options

There are many ways that you can import data into Microsoft Dynamics CRM. Typically in CRM 2011 you had:

1. CRM Import Data Wizard.
2. Custom Code with CRM Web Service (which provides additional capabilities that are not available in the Import Data Wizard).
3. Microsoft family, that is Biztalk Server, SQL Server.
4. A third-party tool, that is Scribe Insight.

The data import is usually a serious piece of work. Before making the decision about how to do it, you need to clearly understand the business requirements. Ask some questions about the frequency of the data import (one time import, on schedule, or on demand), the size of the data, dependencies, and so on. Sometimes you don't even need to use the Data Import services when writing custom code; a simple CRM Create/Update method could solve your problem.

Summary

In this chapter, we introduced the new features of the Import Data Tool. We demonstrated how to import data from one source file (`.csv`) or several source files (`.zip`), as well as how to include Notes and Attachments. We also demonstrated that a source file can contain data for one entity type or for multiple entity types.

We also briefly introduced other data import options.

4
Client-Side Programming

Microsoft Dynamics CRM 2011 has changed the client-side programming model. It introduces a new object model for programming, and adds some new capabilities for showing and hiding user interface elements, supporting multiple forms per entity, and provides new controls for attributes. It also introduces a new file depository called Web Resources. Web Resources changes the way that we associate events to our forms and attributes. In addition to the SOAP end-point in Microsoft Dynamics CRM 4.0, Microsoft CRM 2011 introduces a new architectural style in which every resource is addressed by using a unique URI. This is called REST. In this chapter, we are going to give you an overview of the new client-side programming features that have been added to the product. We are going to cover the following topics:

- What is new in CRM 2011?
- The Xrm.Page Namespace
- SOAP and REST Endpoint
- Advanced Client-Side Programming

What is new in CRM 2011?

Client-side programming offers ways for us to interact with the entity forms by using JScript, through different events provided in Microsoft Dynamics CRM. We often use client-side programming to perform data validation, automation, and process enhancement, because it can provide an immediate response back to the users. Let's walk through the new features.

Web Resources

Web Resources is new in CRM 2011. Web Resources provides a way to store files virtually in the Microsoft Dynamics CRM database, so that we can retrieve them by using a URL address. You may think of Web Resources as a folder on your local computer, and you can create folders within this folder in order to organize your files.

Web Resources, as shown in the following screenshot, contains files that can be used to customize and extend the Microsoft CRM Web application. This includes HTML files, Script, and Silverlight applications. All files in the Web Resources repository can be referenced by using URL syntax. Therefore, you can leverage these files (individual 'web resources') in form customizations, a Sitemap, and/or the ribbon. We will take a deep dive into web resources in details later in this chapter:

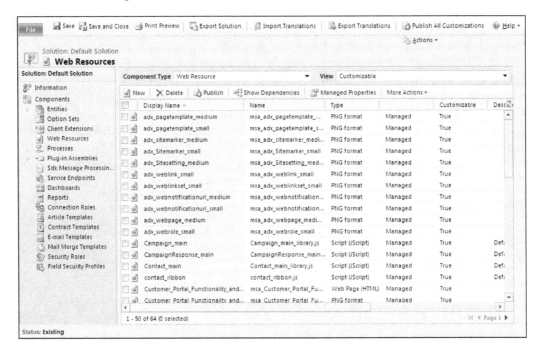

Web resources are stored in a solution. Because web resources are solution components, you can easily export and install them on any Microsoft Dynamics CRM deployment.

Microsoft Dynamics CRM 2011 supports ten file formats. The following table lists each type and the allowed file extensions:

File	File Extensions
Web Page (HTML)	`.htm`, `.html`
Style Sheet (CSS)	`.css`
Script (JScript)	`.js`
Data (XML)	`.xml`
Image (PNG, JPG, GIF, ICO)	`.png`, `.jpg`, `.gif`, `.ico`
Silverlight (XAP)	`.xap`
Style Sheet (XSL)	`.xsl`, `.xslt`

To access the Web Resources repository, follow these steps:

1. Navigate to the **Settings** area.
2. Select **Customizations** from the left-hand navigation menu.
3. Click **Customize the system**.
4. Click on **Web Resources** on the left navigation menu.

 Note: Because Web Resources is one of the solution components, you can also access the Web Resources area in your customized solution.

Creating a new web resource

We will be creating multiple web resources to support the ACM system. To create a new Web Resources, follow these steps:

1. Click **New** on the grid menu.
2. Enter the **Name**.
3. Enter the **Display Name** (optional).
4. Select the **Type** of your Web Resource.
5. Select the **Language** from the drop-down list (optional).
6. Click **Save** on the ribbon to save the web resource.

Consider organizing your web resources in a folder structure using the type of resource that is driving the Web Resource name that you give it. For example you might use the "/scripts" folder structure to store `.js` files. This will help to group the web resources, making them easier to find when you need to manage them, and will also help to make sure that you do not duplicate resources. You may consider using the following folder structure for the project.

- Image: `/images/`
- Script: `/scripts/`
- Style Sheet: `/styles/`
- Icon: `/icons/`
- Data: `/data/`
- Web Page: `/`
- Silverlight: `/`

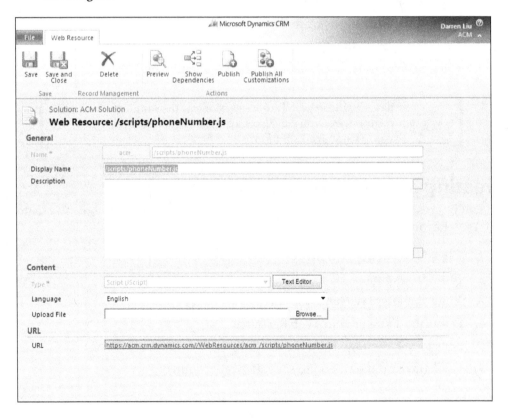

As you can see from the previous screenshot, a URL is generated automatically, so you can access this web resource using the URL.

Referencing a web resource

Once the web resource is created in the Web Resources library, we often need to reference that web resource on a form, ribbon, or Sitemap. There are three approaches that we can leverage: $webresource Directive, Relative URL, and Full URL. Let us walkthrough the steps of inserting a web resource on a form and also take a look at the different approaches to referencing web resources.

To insert a web resource onto a form, following these steps:

1. Navigate to the form designer.
2. Click on the **Insert** tab on the ribbon.
3. Click on the **Web Resource** button in the **Control** group, as shown in the following screenshot:

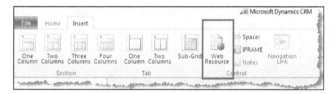

4. In the **Add Web Resource** dialog box, click the **Web source lookup** button to select the web resource in the Web Resource library, and then click the **OK** button:

5. Enter the **Name** and the **Label** for the web resource.

6. Click the **OK** button to insert the web resource onto the form.

Now we know how to insert a web resource onto a form, let's take a look at the different ways for referencing the web resource in the SiteMap, ribbon, and our JScript code.

$webresource directive

You should always use the `$webresource` directive when referencing a web resource from a subarea in the SiteMap or control in the ribbon. To use the `$webresource` directive, use the following syntax:

```
$webresource: <name of Web Resource>
```

 Note: You must use the Name of the web resource and not the Display Name of the web resource. Also remember to include the "prefix" that is appended to the web resource name.

Relative URL

When referencing a web resource from areas that do not support using the `$webresource` directive, you can use a relative URL to reference the web resource. You should always use relative URLs to reference one web resource from another. For example, for the web page web resource `acm_/mypage.htm` to reference the CSS Web resource `acm_/styles/myStyles.css`, you create the link as shown:

```
<link rel="stylesheet" type="text/css"
      href="../styles/myStyles.css" />
```

Full URL

You can also reference a web resource by using its full URL. The sample pattern below indicates how the web resource URL is being assembled:

```
<Microsoft CRM URL>/WebResources/<name of Web resource>
```

 Note: Because Microsoft CRM Server URL is different in each environment, it is recommended to use the `getServerUrl` JScript function to retrieve the Server URL.

Form and Field events

CRM 2011 has all of the form events that CRM 4.0 supports and also has extra events to deal with tabs and IFRAMEs, because CRM 2011 has added tabs to the form and improved the IFRAME capability. In addition, how we usually associate JScript to the form has been changed. Let's take a look at each of the events in detail, and also examine the changes that have been made in Dynamics CRM 2011.

To launch the Form Designer, follow these steps:

1. Navigate to your solution and expand **Entities**.
2. Expand the **Crew Member** entity.
3. Click on **Forms**.

 Note: Microsoft Dynamics CRM 2011 supports multiple forms, as shown in the following screenshot. Double-click on the form that you would like modify in order to apply the event.

4. Double-click the `Main` form to open up the form for editing.

> Tip: If you have privileges to modify the form, you will see a
> **Customize** tab on the ribbon when you open up the Crew Member
> form. Click the **Form** button to open the Form Designer, as shown in
> the next screenshot:

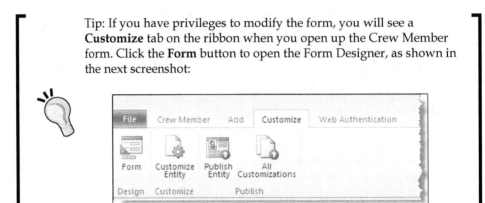

The `OnLoad` event occurs after the form has been loaded. You can use the `OnLoad`
event to apply logic about how the form should be displayed, to set properties on
fields, and to interact with other page elements. Let us walk through an example of
how to apply an `OnLoad` event to the Crew Member entity in the ACM system. Please
follow these steps:

1. Click on **Form Properties** on the ribbon to bring up the Form Properties
    window; please refer to the following screenshots:

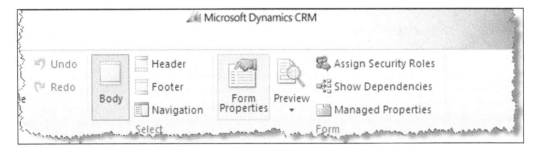

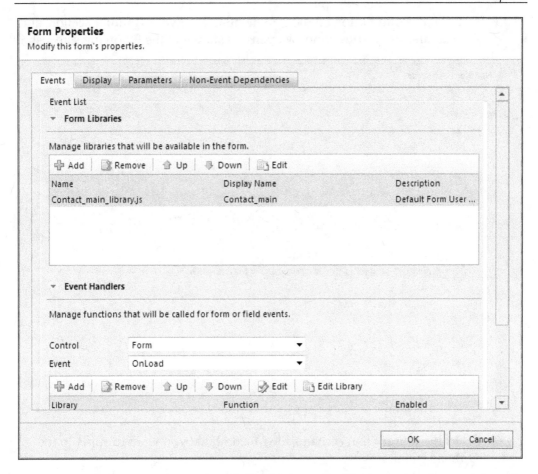

2. Click the **Add** button on the grid menu in the **Form Libraries** section to add the Form Libraries that you are going to use with this form. Form Libraries are the files that are stored in Web Resources, and contain commonly-used JScript functions—for phone number formatting, validation, and so on—that we use across multiple forms.

3. Select **Form** from the **Control** drop-down list.

4. Select **OnLoad** from the **Event** drop-down list.

5. Click on the **Add** button on the grid menu in the **Event Handler** section, and the **Handler Properties** window opens, as shown in the following screenshot:

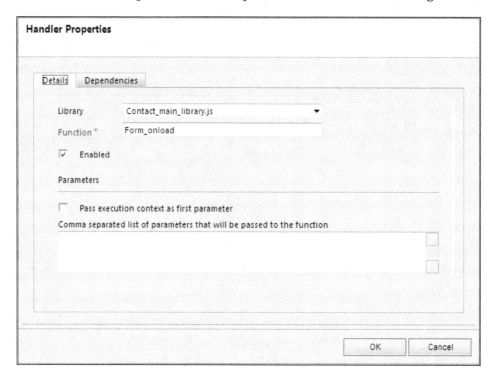

6. Select the **Library** that contains the function that you want to apply to the **OnLoad** event.

7. Enter the **name** of the function in the **Function** field.

Note: If you want to pass the execution context and parameters to the function, then you can select the **Pass execution context as first parameter** option and then enter the parameters, separated by commas in the **Parameters** textbox, We often use the execution context to re-use JScript functions for different events.

8. Click the **OK** button to close the **Handler Properties** window.

The OnSave event occurs when you press the **Save** button or the **Save and Close** buttons. To add an **OnSave** event follow the steps shown in the **OnSave** section, but in the **Form Properties**, select **OnSave** from the **Event** drop-down list, as shown in the following screenshot:

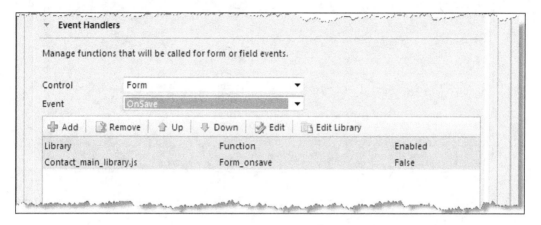

The OnChange event is available for every field on the form. The OnChange event requires two conditions to be true in order for the event to trigger:

1. The data in the field must change.
2. The field must lose focus.

OnChange actions are usually used to change the formatting of fields, such as telephone numbers, validating e-mail addresses, and performing calculations to change other fields based on changing values in one field.

To apply an OnChange event to a field, follow these steps:

1. Double-click on the field on the form to open the **Field Properties** window.
2. Click on the **Events** tab.
3. Add the associated file(s) to the **Form Libraries** section.
4. Select **OnChange** from the **Event** drop-down list, as shown in the next screenshot.

5. Add the **Event Handler** that you would like to associate to the field.

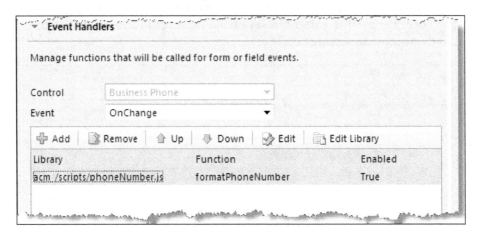

The `TabStateChange` event occurs when a tab is expanded or collapsed. To apply an event to the tab, follow these steps:

1. Double-click on the **Tab** on the form to open up the **Tab Properties** window.

2. Click on the **Events** tab.

3. Add the associated file(s) to the **Form Libraries** section.

4. Select **TabStateChange** from the **Event** drop-down list, as shown in the next screenshot.

5. Add the **Event Handler** that you would like to associate to the tab.

Tip: This event is important if you are using a script to modify the
`src` property of an IFRAME control. An IFRAME will be refreshed
when the tab is expanded. Any changes to the `src` property will be
removed. If you interact with the `src` property of an IFRAME, you
should always include this code in the `TabStateChange` event
instead of the `Onload` event.

The `OnReadyStateComplete` event is used to detect the content of an IFRAME when
it has loaded, and you can access the content using your code. This event provides
a location to include a script that will execute as soon as the content of the IFRAME
has completed loading. To apply an event to an IFRAME, follow these steps:

1. Double-click on the IFRAME on the form, to open the **IFRAME Properties**
   window.
2. Click on the **Events** tab.
3. Add the associated file(s) to the **Form Libraries** section.
4. Select **OnReadyStateComplete** from the **Event** drop-down list, as shown in
   the following screenshot.
5. Add the **Event Handler** that you would like to associate to the IFRAME.

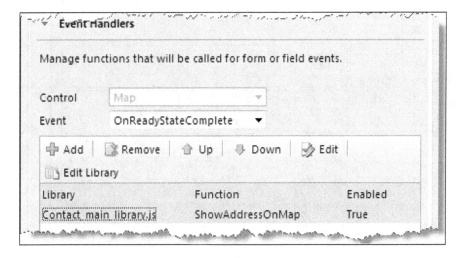

Xrm.Page namespace

In Microsoft Dynamics CRM 4.0, we used the `crmForm` object to gain access to the form fields. The `crmForm` object is deprecated in Microsoft Dynamics CRM 2011. In this version of CRM, a new object model is introduced for form programming, which adds the following capabilities:

- Showing and hiding user interface elements
- Supporting multiple controls per attribute
- Supporting multiple forms per entity
- Manipulating form navigation items

Xrm.Page namespace is a container for three objects: Context, Data, and UI. The **Context** object provides methods to retrieve information specific to an organization, a user, or parameters that were passed to the form in a query string. The **Data** object provides access to the entity data. The **UI** object contains methods to retrieve information about the user interface, in addition to collections for several sub-components of the form. The following diagram shows the Xrm.Page namespace and the objects contained in this namespace:

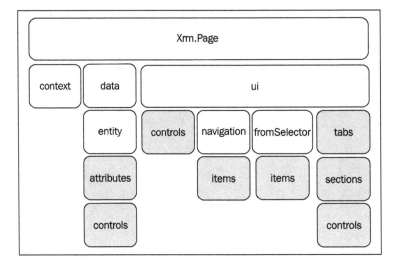

SOAP and REST endpoints

Microsoft Dynamics CRM 2011 has two services available, and each service provides specific strengths when it comes to client-side programming. **SOAP** endpoint is recommended for retrieving metadata, assigning records and executing messages programmatically. **REST** endpoint is recommended for creating, retrieving, updating, and deleting records. It is also recommended for associating and disassociating records. Both of these web services rely on the authentication provided by CRM; the web services are not accessible outside of the application. You can use the web services within JScript libraries, Web Pages, and Silverlight Controls that are stored in Web Resources.

SOAP endpoint

The SOAP endpoint provides access to all of the messages defined in the Organization service. There is no strong type support, and only the types defined within the WSDL will be returned.

The SOAP endpoint uses the Organization service, and the authentication is provided by the application. You can use the SOAP endpoint for Web Resources with JScript libraries or by using Microsoft Silverlight.

Using the SOAP endpoint with JScript

To use the SOAP endpoint with JScript, you need to use XmlHttpRequest to POST requests to the service. The body of the request must contain the XML appropriate for the message that you are using. You must also parse the XML returned in a response. With XmlHttpRequest it is possible to make synchronous requests. However, it is highly recommended to always use asynchronous requests. Because manually configuring each request is very time-consuming, it is expected that you will reuse existing libraries or create your own.

The following JScript sample shows how you can use the SOAP endpoint to assign records in Microsoft Dynamics CRM 2011:

```
if (typeof (SDK) == "undefined")
{ SDK = { __namespace: true }; }
SDK.SOAPSamples = {
  _getServerUrl: function () {
  var OrgServicePath = "/XRMServices/2011/Organization.svc/web";
  var serverUrl = ";
  if (typeof GetGlobalContext == "function") {
    var context = GetGlobalContext();
    serverUrl = context.getServerUrl();   }
  else {
```

```
        if (typeof Xrm.Page.context == "object") {
          serverUrl = Xrm.Page.context.getServerUrl();}
        else
        { throw new Error("Unable to access the server URL"); }
      }
      if (serverUrl.match(/\/$/)) {
        serverUrl = serverUrl.substring(0, serverUrl.length - 1);}
      return serverUrl + OrgServicePath;
    },
      assignRequest: function (Assignee, Target, Type, successCallback,
        errorCallback) {
      var request = "<s:Envelope
        xmlns:s=\"http://schemas.xmlsoap.org/soap/envelope/\">";
      request += "<s:Body>";
      request += "<Execute
        xmlns=\"http://schemas.microsoft.com/xrm/2011/Contracts/
        Services\";
      request += " xmlns:i=\"http://www.w3.org/2001/XMLSchema-
        instance\">";
      request += <request i:type=\"b:AssignRequest\";
      request += "
        xmlns:a=\"http://schemas.microsoft.com/xrm/2011/Contracts\";
      request += "
        xmlns:b=\"http://schemas.microsoft.com/crm/2011/Contracts\">";
      request += "<a:Parameters
        xmlns:c=\"http://schemas.datacontract.org/2004/07/System.
        Collections.Generic\">";
      request += "<a:KeyValuePairOfstringanyType>";
      request += "<c:key>Target</c:key>";
      request += "<c:value i:type=\"a:EntityReference\">";
      request += "<a:Id>" + Target + "</a:Id>";
      request += "<a:LogicalName>" + Type + "</a:LogicalName>";
      request += "<a:Name i:nil=\"true\" />";
      request += "</c:value>";
      request += "</a:KeyValuePairOfstringanyType>";
      request += "<a:KeyValuePairOfstringanyType>";
      request += "<c:key>Assignee</c:key>";
      request += "<c:value i:type=\"a:EntityReference\">";
      request += "<a:Id>" + Assignee + "</a:Id>";
      request += "<a:LogicalName>systemuser</a:LogicalName>";
      request += "<a:Name i:nil=\"true\" />";
      request += "</c:value>";
      request += "</a:KeyValuePairOfstringanyType>";
      request += "</a:Parameters>";
      request += "<a:RequestId i:nil=\"true\" />";
```

```
request += "<a:RequestName>Assign</a:RequestName>";
request += "</request>";
request += "</Execute>";
request += "</s:Body>";
request += "</s:Envelope>";

var req = new XMLHttpRequest();
req.open("POST", SDK.SOAPSamples._getServerUrl(), true)
req.setRequestHeader("Accept", "application/xml, text/xml,
  */*");
req.setRequestHeader("Content-Type", "text/xml; charset=utf-
  8");
req.setRequestHeader("SOAPAction",
  "http://schemas.microsoft.com/xrm/2011/Contracts/Services
  /IOrganizationService/Execute");
req.onreadystatechange = function () {
  SDK.SOAPSamples.assignResponse(req, successCallback,
  errorCallback); };
req.send(request); },
assignResponse: function (req, successCallback, errorCallback) {
  if (req.readyState == 4) {
    if (req.status == 200) {
      if (successCallback != null)
      { successCallback(); }
    }
    else {
      errorCallback(SDK.SOAPSamples._getError(req.responseXML)); }
  }
},
_getError: function (faultXml) {
  var errorMessage = "Unknown Error (Unable to parse the fault)";
  if (typeof faultXml == "object") {
    try {
      var bodyNode = faultXml.firstChild.firstChild;
      for (var i = 0; i < bodyNode.childNodes.length; i++) {
        var node = bodyNode.childNodes[i];

        if ("s:Fault" == node.nodeName) {
          for (var j = 0; j < node.childNodes.length; j++) {
            var faultStringNode = node.childNodes[j];
            if ("faultstring" == faultStringNode.nodeName) {
              errorMessage = faultStringNode.text;
              break; }
          }
          break;
```

```
            }
          }
        }
      catch (e) { };
    }
    return new Error(errorMessage);
  },
  __namespace: true
};
```

Using the SOAP endpoint with Silverlight

To use the SOAP endpoint with Silverlight, you need to adhere to the following guidelines after your project is created:

1. Add a service reference to the Organization service.

 Note: The URL of the service is located on the Developer Resources page of Microsoft Dynamics CRM 2011. In the **Settings** area, select **Customizations**, and then select **Developer Resources**.

2. Add some additional files to your solution, and manually modify the `Reference.cs` file that is generated when you add the service reference.
3. Write code using asynchronous methods.
4. Use the late binding syntax, because strong types are not available.

REST endpoint

REST is the abbreviation for **Representational State Transfer**. You can use the REST endpoint to execute HTTP requests by using a service that is based on a URI. REST works the way the Internet works. You interact with resources by using HTTP verbs such as GET, POST, MERGE, and DELETE. Various libraries can be used to process the HTTP requests and responses. REST allows for synchronous and asynchronous processing of operations. The capability to perform asynchronous operations makes REST a good fit for Silverlight clients.

Microsoft Dynamics CRM 2011 uses the WCF Data Services framework to provide an OData endpoint that is a REST-based data service. The endpoint is called the Organization Data Service. The Organization Data Service root URI is:

```
[Your Organization Root URL]/xrmservices/2011/organizationdata.svc
```

To provide a consistent set of URIs that correspond to the entities used in Microsoft Dynamics CRM, an Entity Data Model organizes the form of records of "entity types" and the ones associated between them. The Entity Data Model in OData Service Metadata document is available at:

```
[Your Organization Root URL]/xrmservices/2011/organizationdata.
svc/$metadata
```

Because the REST endpoint cannot perform the Execute operation, it is the recommended web service for tasks that involve creating, retrieving, updating, and deleting records.

Let's take a look at a sample to create, retrieve, update, and delete records using the REST endpoint.

The following code demonstrates how to use the REST endpoint to create a Crew Member in the ACM system:

```
function createContactRecord(firstName, lastName) {
    showMessage("createContactRecord function START");
    var Contact = new Object();
    Contact.FirstName = firstName;
    Contact.LastName = lastName;
    var jsonContact = window.JSON.stringify(Contact);

    var createContactReq = new XMLHttpRequest();
    createContactReq.open("POST", ODataPath + "/ContactSet", true);
    createContactReq.setRequestHeader("Accept", "application/json");
    createContactReq.setRequestHeader("Content-Type",
      "application/json;
    charset=utf-8");
    createContactReq.onreadystatechange = function () {
      createContactReqCallBack(this);
    };
    createContactReq.send(jsonContact);
    showMessage("createContactRecord function END");
}

function createContactReqCallBack(createContactReq) {
    if (createContactReq.readyState == 4 /* complete */) {
      if (createContactReq.status == 201) {
      //Success
      var newContact = JSON.parse(createContactReq.responseText).d;
      showMessage("ACTION: Created new Contact id:{" +
        newContact.ContactId + "}.");
```

```
        //NEXT STEP: Retrieve the Contact
        retrieveContactRecord(newContact.ContactId);
        showMessage("createContactReqCallBack function success END");
      }
      else {
        //Failure
        errorHandler(createContactReq);
        showMessage("createContactReqCallBack function failure END");
      }
    }
  }
};
```

The following code demonstrates how to use the REST endpoint to retrieve a Crew Member in the ACM system:

```
function retrieveContactRecord(Id) {
  showMessage("retrieveContactRecord function START");

  var retrieveContactReq = new XMLHttpRequest();
  retrieveContactReq.open("GET", ODataPath + "/ContactSet(
    guid'" + Id + "')", true);
  retrieveContactReq.setRequestHeader("Accept", "application/json");
  retrieveContactReq.setRequestHeader("Content-Type",
    "application/json; charset=utf-8");
  retrieveContactReq.onreadystatechange = function () {
  retrieveContactReqCallBack(this);
  };
  retrieveContactReq.send();
  showMessage("retrieveContactRecord function END.");
}


function retrieveContactReqCallBack(retrieveContactReq) {
  if (retrieveContactReq.readyState == 4 /* complete */) {
    if (retrieveContactReq.status == 200) {
    //Success
      var retrievedContact =
        JSON.parse(retrieveContactReq.responseText).d;
      showMessage("ACTION: Retrieved Contact Name = \"" +
        retrievedContact.FullName + "\", ContactId = {" +
        retrievedContact.ContactId + "}");

      //NEXT STEP: Update the Contact
      updateContactRecord(retrievedContact.ContactId);
      showMessage("retrieveContactReqCallBack function success END");
    }
```

```
        else {
         //Failure
         errorHandler(retrieveContactReq);
         showMessage("retrieveContactReqCallBack function failure END");
        }
      }
    }
```

The following code demonstrates how to use the REST endpoint to update a Crew Member in the ACM system:

```
function updateContactRecord(Id) {
  showMessage("updateContactRecord function START");
  var updateContactReq = new XMLHttpRequest();
  var changes = new Object();
  changes.FirstName = "Darren";
  changes.FirstName = "Liu";
  changes.Telephone1 = "555-0123";
  changes.EMailAddress1 = "someone1@example.com";

  updateContactReq.open("POST", ODataPath + "/ContactSet(
    guid'" + Id + "')", true);
  updateContactReq.setRequestHeader("Accept", "application/json");
  updateContactReq.setRequestHeader("Content-Type",
    "application/json; charset=utf-8");
  updateContactReq.setRequestHeader("X-HTTP-Method", "MERGE");
  updateContactReq.onreadystatechange = function () {
    updateContactReqCallBack(this, Id);
  };
  updateContactReq.send(JSON.stringify(changes));
  showMessage("updateContactRecord function END.");
}


function updateContactReqCallBack(updateContactReq, Id) {
  if (updateContactReq.readyState == 4 /* complete */) {
    //There appears to be an issue where IE maps the 204 status
      to 1223 when no content is returned.
    if (updateContactReq.status == 204 ||
      updateContactReq.status == 1223) {
      //Success
      showMessage("ACTION: Updated Contact data.");

      //NEXT STEP: Delete the Contact
      deleteContactRecord(Id);
      showMessage("updateContactReqCallBack function success END");
```

```
      }
      else {
        //Failure
        errorHandler(updateContactReq);
        showMessage("updateContactReqCallBack function failure END");
      }
    }
  }
}
```

The following code demonstrates how to use the REST endpoint to delete a Crew Member in the ACM system:

```
function deleteContactReqCallBack(deleteContactReq) {
  if (deleteContactReq.readyState == 4 /* complete */) {
    //There appears to be an issue where IE maps the 204
      status to 1223 when no content is returned.
    if (deleteContactReq.status == 204 ||
      deleteContactReq.status == 1223) {
      //Success
      showMessage("ACTION: The Contact record was deleted.");
      showMessage("deleteContactReqCallBack function success END");
    }
    else {
      //Failure
      errorHandler(deleteContactReq);
      showMessage("deleteContactReqCallBack function failure END");
    }
  }
}
```

There are many other things that you can do with the SOAP and REST Endpoints. The new programming model also provides developers with other functionality for client-side programming. The new features allow all of us to take CRM customization to the next level.

There are more sample codes in the Microsoft Dynamics CRM 2011 Software Development Kit(SDK). To download the Microsoft Dynamics CRM 2011 SDK, visit the Microsoft Download Center at http://www.microsoft.com/download/en/details.aspx?id=24004.

Summary

In this chapter, we have covered the features that were added to Microsoft Dynamics CRM 2011. You should be familiar with Web Resources, the new way of associating events to form elements, the Xrm.Page namespace, and the SOAP and REST Endpoints provided to you. Now you can perform more client-side customizations with the new features added in Microsoft Dynamics CRM 2011.

In the next chapter, we are going to take a look at some of the new server-side features of Microsoft Dynamics CRM 2011.

Server-Side Programming

5

Microsoft Dynamics CRM 2011 provides powerful, event-driven, server-side programming methods: Plug-ins and Processes (Formerly Workflows). In this chapter, we will:

- Highlight both methods, compare the differences, and provide some code examples for our ACM system.
- Introduce the CRM 2011 Event Framework, Web Services methods and messages, Early Bound Entity Classes, and Late Bound Entity Classes.
- Introduce the new CRM 2011 Dialog: a wizard-like, synchronous process.

For detailed information about Plug-ins and Processes, please refer to the SDK.

CRM Web Services and Assemblies

There are two ways to use CRM services in code: SDK assemblies and service references. Using SDK assemblies is the recommended approach for Microsoft Dynamics CRM 2011 development. So in this chapter, we will only introduce how to use SDK assemblies to access CRM data.

CRM Web Services methods and messages

Microsoft Dynamics CRM 2011 provides two major Web Services:

1. **IOrganizationService**: The primary CRM Web Service used to access data and metadata for the specified organization.

The following diagram shows the methods and messages of IOrganizationService:

Common methods
- *a set of methods used to perform the most common operations on system and custom entities.*
Method

Create
Retrieve
RetrieveMultiple
Update
Delete
Associate
Disassociate
Message

AssociateRequest
CreateRequest
DeleteRequest
DisassociateRequest
RetrieveRequest
RetrieveMultipleRequest
UpdateRequest
Data Message

XRM Messages - *The Microsoft.Xrm.Sdk.Messages namespace supports the core messages used to work with the data stored in any entity. This namespace also contains the messages you can use to retrieve and customize the metadata for entities, attributes, and relationships.*

CanBeReferencedRequest
CanBeReferencingRequest
CanManyToManyRequest
CreateAttributeRequest
CreateEntityRequest
CreateManyToManyRequest
CreateOneToManyRequest
CreateOptionSetRequest
DeleteAttributeRequest
DeleteEntityRequest
DeleteOptionSetRequest
DeleteOptionValueRequest
DeleteRelationshipRequest
GetValidManyToManyRequest
GetValidReferencedEntitiesRequest
GetValidReferencingEntitiesRequest
InsertOptionValueRequest
InsertStatusValueRequest
OrderOptionRequest
RetrieveAllEntitiesRequest
RetrieveAttributeRequest
RetrieveEntityRequest
RetrieveOptionSetRequest
RetrieveRelationshipRequest
RetrieveTimestampRequest
UpdateAttributeRequest
UpdateEntityRequest
UpdateOptionSetRequest
UpdateOptionValueRequest
UpdateRelationshipRequest
UpdateStateValueRequest
Metadata Message

IOrganizationService
Provides programmatic access to the metadata and data for an organization.
Namespace: Microsoft.Xrm.Sdk
Assembly: Microsoft.Xrm.Sdk (in microsoft.xrm.sdk.dll)
Web Service

Execute methods
- *a set of methods used to perform the most common operations on system and custom entities and on the metadata for your organization.*
Method

CRM Messages - *The Microsoft.Crm.Sdk.Messages namespace contains all the messages you need to work with the data stored in any entity. The solution messages are also in this namespace.*

223 Requests Messages...
Message

2. **IDiscoveryService**: Useful in a multi-tenant environment to determine whether a user is a member of the organization, and the endpoint address URL used to access the IOrganizationService Web Service for each of the organizations.

The following diagram shows the methods and messages of IDiscoverService:

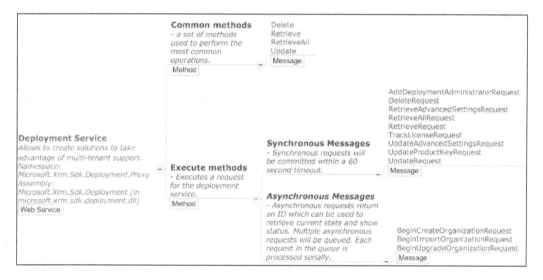

In addition to the above Web Services, CRM also provides a multi-tenant support Web Service: **IDeploymentService**. This capability benefits hosted solutions or businesses that require a separation of data inside the organization.

The following diagram shows the methods and messages of IDeploymentService:

The following table lists CRM Service References Endpoints (from the CRM SDK):

Services	Description
Discovery Service	The IDiscoveryService Web Service provides information about the organizations available on the Microsoft Dynamics CRM server using the SOAP protocol.
For CRM On-premises	`http://ServerName/XRMServices/2011/Discovery.svc`
For CRM Online	`https://dev.crm.dynamics.com/XRMServices/2011/Discovery.svc (North America)`
	`https://dev.crm4.dynamics.com/XRMServices/2011/Discovery.svc (EMEA)`
	`https://dev.crm5.dynamics.com/XRMServices/2011/Discovery.svc (APAC)`
Organization Service	The IOrganizationService Web service provides access to the business data and metadata of your organization by using the SOAP protocol
For CRM On-premises	`http://ServerName/OrganizationName/XRMServices/2011/Organization.svc`
For CRM Online	`https://OrganizationName.api.crm.dynamics.com/XrmServices/2011/Organization.svc (North America)`
	`https://OrganizationName.api.crm4.dynamics.com/XrmServices/2011/Organization.svc (EMEA)`
	`https://OrganizationName.api.crm5.dynamics.com/XrmServices/2011/Organization.svc (APAC)`
Organization Data Service	This **Open Data (OData)** Web service provides access to the business data of your organization by exposing a RESTful API
For CRM On-premises	`http://ServerName/OrganizationName/XRMServices/2011/OrganizationData.svc`
For CRM Online	`https://OrganizationName.api.crm.dynamics.com/XrmServices/2011/OrganizationData.svc (North America)`
	`https://OrganizationName.api.crm4.dynamics.com/XrmServices/2011/OrganizationData.svc (EMEA)`
	`https://OrganizationName.api.crm5.dynamics.com/XrmServices/2011/OrganizationData.svc (APAC)`
Deployment Service	`http://myservername/xrmdeployment/2011/deployment.svc`

To use the CRM Web Services, add the Microsoft Dynamics CRM 2011 Assemblies (.dll files) to the Visual Studio project (best practice); alternatively, add the Service Reference to your project.

SDK Assemblies

The following table lists CRM SDK Assemblies (from the CRM SDK):

Assembly and Namespace	Description
Microsoft.Crm.Sdk.Proxy.dll	Defines requests and responses for messages, business data model specific (non-core) messages, as well as enumerations required for working with organization data
Microsoft.Crm.Sdk	Contains enumerations of possible picklists and integer values for some attributes. The naming convention of the classes is <EntityName><AttributeName>, to make it easier to locate the specific attribute
Microsoft.Crm.Sdk.Messages	Contains request and responses for business data model specific (non-core) messages
Microsoft.Xrm.Sdk.dll	Defines the core xRM methods and types, including proxy classes to make the connection to CRM simpler, authentication methods, and the service contracts
Microsoft.Xrm.Sdk	Defines the data contracts for attribute types, interfaces for authoring Plug-ins, and other general purpose xRM types and methods
Microsoft.Xrm.Sdk.Client	Defines classes for use by client code, including a data context, proxy classes to ease the connection to Microsoft Dynamics CRM, and the LINQ provider
Microsoft.Xrm.Sdk.Discovery	Defines all classes required to communicate with the Discovery Service, including the service contract, all request/responses, and supporting classes
Microsoft.Xrm.Sdk.Messages	Defines request/response classes for Create, Retrieve, Update, Delete, Associate, Disassociate, and the metadata classes
Microsoft.Xrm.Sdk.Metadata	Defines the data contracts for Microsoft Dynamics CRM metadata
Microsoft.Xrm.Sdk.Query	Defines query classes required to connect to Microsoft Dynamics CRM

Assembly and Namespace	Description
Microsoft.Xrm.Sdk.Workflow.dll	Defines types and methods required to author a custom workflow activity
Microsoft.Xrm.Sdk.Workflow	Defines the attribute and dependency property classes required to author a custom workflow activity
Microsoft.Xrm.Sdk.Workflow.Activities	Defines the workflow activities that are used by the Microsoft Dynamics CRM workflow designer
Microsoft.Xrm.Sdk.Workflow.Designers	Defines a Visual Studio designer for displaying a Microsoft Dynamics CRM workflow in Visual Studio
Microsoft.Crm.Tools.EmailProviders.dll	Defines methods and types needed for developing a custom e-mail provider component for the Microsoft Dynamics CRM E-mail Router
Microsoft.Crm.Tools.Email.Management	Defines the e-mail provider management types
Microsoft.Crm.Tools.Email.Providers	Defines the base class for a custom e-mail provider and supporting types
Microsoft.Xrm.Sdk.Deployment.dll	Defines types and methods for interacting with the Deployment Web Service
Microsoft.Xrm.Sdk.Deployment	Defines the data contracts necessary to communicate with the Deployment Web Service
Microsoft.Xrm.Sdk.Deployment.Proxy	Defines a helper class to generate a proxy for the Deployment Web Service

Early-Bound and Late-Bound

Both Early-Bound and Late-Bound are programming types in Microsoft Dynamics CRM. The Early-Bound type provides strong type support, and all type references are checked at compile time. By contrast, Late-Bound is loosely typed, and checks types only when the object is created or an action is performed on the type. As a best practice, use Early-Bound types where possible (that is, entities/attributes are already defined at the coding time) to save the compile time verification of entity and attribute names.

To use Early-Binding: Use code generation tools (CrmSvcUtil.exe) to generate an Early-Bound class file and include it in the project. The class file has the following features:

1. The class file contains all CRM entities, attributes, and relationships (one class per entity);

2. The class file needs to be regenerated each time the system is customized.

3. The classes can be used in any project type, or built into a class library.

Early-Binding Example:

```
acm_flight flight = newacm_flight();
flight.acm_name = "AA100 @ 2011-06-01.13:21";
```

Use Late-Binding if the code needs to work with unknown entities/attributes at coding time, that is, a generic ISV solution.

To use Late-Binding: Use the Entity class, which is the base class for all types of entities in Microsoft Dynamics CRM. This class defines a collection of attributes that can be used to get and set the values of attributes. When initialized, the Entity class contains the logical name of an entity and a property-bag array of the entity's attributes. To use this model, the exact logical name must be known (and specified) as a string.

Late-Binding Example:

```
Entityacm_flight = newEntity("acm_flight");
acm_flight["name"] = "AA100 @ 2011-06-01.13:21";
```

 Note: When developing a Plug-in, all Entity values that are assigned to `IPluginExecutionContext` must be late-bound types.

Data queries

There are several ways to query CRM data, in addition of support FetchXML and QueryExpression, Microsoft Dynamics CRM 2011 also supports the .NET Language-Integrated Query (LINQ) to query CRM data; LINQ uses standard query patterns, but internally it uses QueryExpression, so it is limited to the features of QueryExpression that doesn't support aggregates and grouping. FetchXML supports all the features of QueryExpression, plus aggregates and grouping.

Here's a sample code that uses CRM Assemblies, LINQ, and Early Bounding to list all flights and its crewmembers (flight and crewmember are connected through the Connection Entity).

 In the sample code, we use an SDK helper class to perform the server connection and user authentication. So we can focus on the business logic.

1. Create a blank solution in Visual Studio 2010, and then add a new console application project called: CRMDataQuery, base on .NET Framework 4, C#.

2. Add assemblies references (located in the SDK\bin folder of the SDK):

    - microsoft.xrm.sdk.dll
    - microsoft.crm.sdk.proxy.dll

3. Add .Net reference:

    - System.ServiceModel
    - System.Runtime.Serialization

4. Run crmsvcutil.exe command to generate strongly-typed classes for the entities in the ACM organization, for early bounding:

5. Run the crmsvcutil.exe command to generate strongly-typed classes for the entities in the ACM organization, for early binding:

    ```
    \sdk\bin>crmsvcutil.exe /url:http://bps:5555/ACM/XRMServices/2011/
    Organization.svc /out:GeneratedCode.cs
    ```

6. Include the GeneratedCode.cs into the project:

 You need to change the **Target framework** in the project property to **.Net Framework 4**, instead of using the **Net Framework 4 Client Profile** by default.

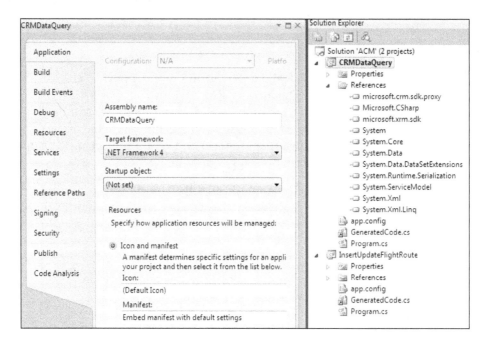

7. The `Program.cs` is the `Main()` method class, it does the query work in CRM, lists all flights and its crewmembers. See the following code:

```
using System;
using System.Collections.Generic;
using System.Linq;
using System.Text;
using System.ServiceModel.Description;
using System.Net;
using Microsoft.Xrm.Sdk.Client;
using Microsoft.Xrm.Sdk;

namespace CRMDataQuery
{
  class Program
  {
    static void Main(string[] args)
    {
      Uri OrganizationUri = new
                          Uri("http://bps:5555/ACM/XRMServices
                          /2011/Organization.svc");
      Uri HomeRealmUri = null;
      ClientCredentials Credentials = new ClientCredentials();
      Credentials.Windows.ClientCredential =
                CredentialCache.DefaultNetworkCredentials;

      try
      {
        //Initializes a new instance of the CRM
          OrganizationServiceProxy class.
        using (OrganizationServiceProxy serviceProxy = new
              OrganizationServiceProxy(OrganizationUri,
              HomeRealmUri, Credentials, null))
        {
          //This statement is required to enable early-bound type
            support.
          serviceProxy.EnableProxyTypes();
          IOrganizationService service =
                            (IOrganizationService)serviceProxy;

          //Create the OrganizationServiceContext object that will
            generate the IQueryable collections for LINQ calls.
          OrganizationServiceContext context = new
                            OrganizationServiceContext(service);

          //Get all flight records that created after 2011-02-22.
          var flights = (from f in
                    context.CreateQuery<acm_flight>()
                    where f.CreatedOn >= new DateTime(2011,02,22)
                    select new
```

```
                    {
                        FlightId = f.Id,
                        FlightName = f.acm_name
                    });

            //Get all crewmembers for each flight.
            foreach (var flight in flights)
            {
                Console.WriteLine("========== Flight Information
                                ==========");
                Console.WriteLine("Flight: {0}", flight.FlightName);
                Console.WriteLine("---------- Crew In This Flight ----
                                ------");

                //You can either query against record1id or record2id
                    - CRM will find all connections that the entity is a
                    part of.
                var crew = (from c in context.CreateQuery<Contact>()
                            join co in
                            context.CreateQuery<Connection>() on c.Id
                            equals co.Record1Id.Id
                            join cr in
                            context.CreateQuery<ConnectionRole>() on
                            co.Record1RoleId.Id equals cr.Id
                            where co.Record2Id.Id == flight.FlightId
                            where cr.Category.Value == 100000000
                            //Category="Flight Crew"
                            orderby c.FullName
                            select new
                            {
                                FullName = c.FullName,
                                RoleName = cr.Name
                            });

            foreach (var member in crew)
            {
                Console.WriteLine("{0} , {1}", member.FullName,
                                member.RoleName);
            }

            Console.WriteLine("");
            }
        }
    }
    catch (Exception ex)
    {
        errorHandler(ex);
    }

    Console.ReadLine();
```

```
    }

    //Display Errors.
    private static void errorHandler(Exception ex)
    {
        Console.WriteLine(ex.Message + ex.InnerException);
        //Console.ReadLine();
    }
  }
}
```

Plug-ins

With Plug-ins we can extend or customize the functionality of the Microsoft Dynamics CRM platform by integrating the custom business logic (code). Plug-ins are triggered by the message with which they're registered on the Microsoft Dynamics CRM platform.

For example, we can register a Plug-in to perform some business logic every time a Flight record is created. We can also define whether to run the business logic BEFORE the Flight record is saved in the CRM organization database (Pre-Event) or AFTER the Flight record is saved in the CRM organization database (Post-Event).

Notice that some of the business logic can also be accomplished with JavaScript, which is a Client-Side programming method, such as data validation or user interface design, and so on. The Client-Side script depends on the user's browser and is triggered by the CRM form events. By contrast, the plug-ins are triggered by the platform events — that is, importing bulk Flight records can trigger Plug-in events, but doesn't trigger the form events.

CRM 2011 allows Plug-ins to participate in SQL transactions, and allows them to create traces returned with exceptions. In the previous version of CRM Online, we cannot deploy Plug-ins and custom workflow activities to the environment. The current version of CRM 2011 supports the execution of Plug-ins in an isolated environment. In this isolated environment, also known as a sandbox, a Plug-in can make use of the full power of the CRM SDK to access the Web Services, in order to perform custom business logic. However, placing Plug-ins in a sandbox prevents you from accessing the file systems, system event log, registries, and network resources. However, sandbox Plug-ins do have access to the external endpoints like the Windows Azure cloud.

Event framework

Microsoft Dynamics CRM 2011 and Microsoft Dynamics CRM Online provide the ability to add custom business logic to the event pipeline on the Microsoft Dynamics CRM server. We call this the event framework. The event framework allows developers to create rich solutions on top of Microsoft CRM, and provides the following key features:

- An improved event processing subsystem that provides a unified method of executing both Plug-ins and workflow activities

- An event framework API for extending the CRM platform through the development of custom business logic in the form of Plug-ins and workflow activities

- Enables the deployment of Plug-in and custom workflow activities to the Microsoft Dynamics CRM database

- Backward compatibility for Microsoft Dynamics CRM 4.0 Plug-ins

- Synchronous and asynchronous execution of Plug-ins

The Plug-ins execute in the Event Framework based on a message pipeline execution model. This can be registered in either synchronous mode or asynchronous mode. The CRM platform core operation and any Plug-ins registered for synchronous execution are executed immediately (executed in a well-defined order). Plug-ins registered for asynchronous execution are queued with the Asynchronous Service in Microsoft Dynamics CRM, and executed at a later time. The following diagram shows the event execution pipeline for Plug-ins:

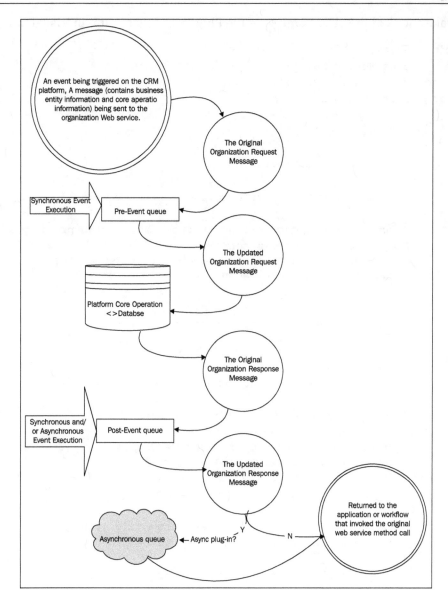

Developing a Plug-in

On the code level, a Plug-in is a custom class that implements the IPlugin interface. A Plug-in can be written in any .NET Framework 4 CLR-compliant language, such as C# and VB .NET in Microsoft Visual Studio 2010. Typical Plug-ins access the information in the context, perform the required business operations, and handle exceptions.

Let's take a look at the SDK example of the Plug-in code structure in Visual Studio:

```
using System;
usingSystem.ServiceModel;
usingSystem.Runtime.Serialization;
usingMicrosoft.Xrm.Sdk;

namespacePluginsSample
{
  public class Class1:IPlugin
  {
    public void Execute(IServiceProviderserviceProvider)
    {
      // Obtain the execution context from the service provider.
      IPluginExecutionContext context = (
        IPluginExecutionContext)serviceProvider.GetService(
        typeof(IPluginExecutionContext));

      // Get a reference to the organization service.
      IOrganizationServiceFactory factory = (
        IOrganizationServiceFactory)serviceProvider.GetService(
        typeof(IOrganizationServiceFactory));
      IOrganizationService service =
        factory.CreateOrganizationService(context.UserId);

      // Get a reference to the tracing service.
      ITracingServicetracingService = (
        ITracingService)serviceProvider.GetService(
        typeof(ITracingService));

      try
      {
        // Plug-in business logic goes below this line.
        // Invoke organization service methods.
      }
      catch (FaultException<OrganizationServiceFault> ex)
      {
        // Handle the exception.
      }
    }
  }
}
```

DLL references

Add Microsoft.Xrm.Sdk.dll and Microsoft.Crm.Sdk.Proxy.dll assembly references to the CRM project, in order to access the CRM context, and then compile the Plug-in code. In addition to these two, you can also reference the following out-of-the-box CRM server DLLs for different purposes:

- Microsoft.Xrm.Sdk.Workflow.dll
- Microsoft.Xrm.Sdk.Deployment.dll
- Microsoft.Crm.Outlook.Sdk.dll
- Microsoft.Crm.Tools.EmailProviders.dll

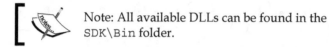 Note: All available DLLs can be found in the SDK\Bin folder.

IPluginInterface and the Execute method

The IPlugin is the base interface for all Plug-ins. The Execute method is also a required method for all Plug-ins. The IServiceProvider parameter of the Execute method is a container for several objects that can be accessed within a Plug-in. The serviceProvider is an instance of the IServiceProvider, which contains references to the execution context (IPluginExecutionContext), IOrganizationServiceFactory, ITracingService, and so on.

- **The IPluginExecutionContext** interface contains information that describes the run-time environment that the plug-in is executing in, information related to the execution pipeline, and entity business information
- **The IOrganizationService** interface provides programmatic access to the metadata and data for an organization
- **The IOrganizationServiceFactory** interface represents a factory for creating IOrganizationService instances
- **The ITracingService** interface provides a method of logging run-time trace information for Plug-ins

Input and output parameters

The **InputParameters** property contains the data that is in the request message that triggered the event that caused the Plug-in to execute.

The **OutputParameters** property contains the data that is in the response message, after the core platform operation has completed.

> Note: Only synchronous post-event and asynchronous registered Plug-ins have OutputParameters populated.

```
// The InputParameters collection contains all the data passed
// in the message request.
if (context.InputParameters.Contains("Target") &&
  context.InputParameters["Target"] is Entity)
{
  // Obtain the target entity from the input parmameters.
  Entity entity = (Entity)context.InputParameters["Target"];
```

Pre and post entity images

PreEntityImages contain the primary entity's attributes (that are set to a value or null) before the core platform operation begins.

PostEntityImages contain the primary entity's attributes (that are set to a value or null) after the core platform operation.

> Note: Only synchronous post-event and asynchronous registered Plug-ins have PostEntityImages populated.

Security

Each Plug-in assembly must be signed either by Visual Studio or by the Strong Name tool. As a best practice, do not develop Plug-in code that contains any system logon information, confidential information, or company trade secrets.

A Plug-in example

Now that we have covered the essential knowledge of the Microsoft Dynamics CRM 2011 Server-Side programming. There is a lot of detailed information in the CRM SDK; please refer to it for a more comprehensive understanding.

It's time to start building a Plug-in example for the ACM system; it will be a Sandbox mode assembly, because we are using Microsoft Dynamics CRM 2011 Online.

The requirement is simple; we want to create a compensation record for each Flight Crew member who served on the flight. Because Flight and Flight Crews are connected through the "Connection" entity (by doing that you can set roles to individuals), we can say: create a compensation record for each connection record created for Flight and Flight Crews with the correct connection roles. The following diagram describes the structure of Connection Roles:

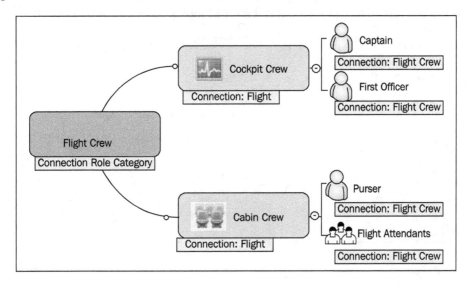

First of all, create a new Connection Role Category. Go to **ACM Solutions | Option Sets | Add Existing**, and then select **Category** (connectionrole_category). Next, go to **ACM Solutions | Option Sets**, double-click on **Category**, and then add a new option called "Flight Crew".

Next, create several Connection Roles. Go to the **ACM Solutions | Connection Roles**, and click the **New** button to create the following roles in the "Flight Crew" category that we have created.

Name	Record Type	Matching Roles	Connection Role Category
Cockpit Crew	Flight	Captain; First Officer	Flight Crew
Cabin Crew	Flight	Purser; Flight Attendant	
Captain	Flight Crew	Cockpit Crew	
First Officer	Flight Crew	Cockpit Crew	
Purser	Flight Crew	Cabin Crew	
Flight Attendant	Flight Crew	Cabin Crew	

The following screenshot shows what it should look like in the end:

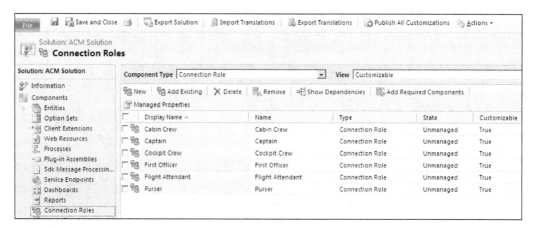

 Note: Each connection will create two connection records in the database: a "Connect From" and a "Connect To".

A Flight can have many connections that connect to CrewMembers to different roles. See the following screenshot as an example:

The following screenshot describes the relationships between Flight, Crew, and Compensation:

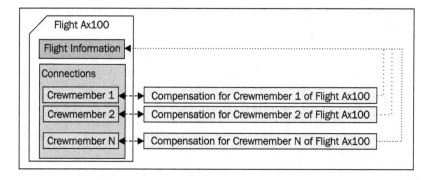

The following diagram shows the process flow for this plug-in:

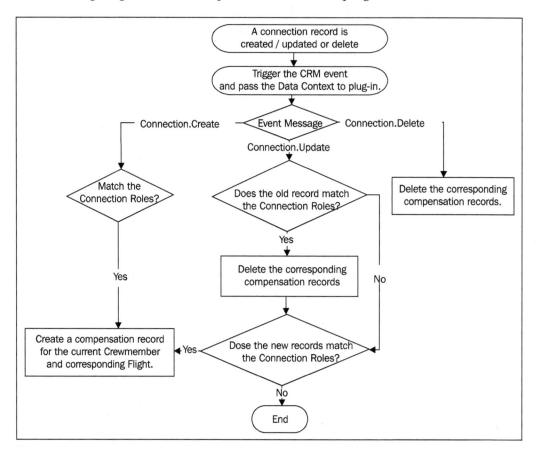

Please carry out the following steps to create a CRM 2011 Plug-in and register the Plug-in on the Create, Update, and Delete message of the Connection entity:

1. Create a new Class Library solution in Visual Studio 2010 called: CompensationGeneration, based on the .NET Framework 4, C#.

2. Add assemblies references (located in the SDK\bin folder of the SDK):
   - microsoft.xrm.sdk.dll
   - microsoft.crm.sdk.proxy.dll

3. Add .Net references:
   - System.Runtime.Serialization
   - System.ServiceModel

4. Right-click **CompensationGeneration** on the Solution Explorer, select **Property**, and then go to **Signing | Sign the assembly**:

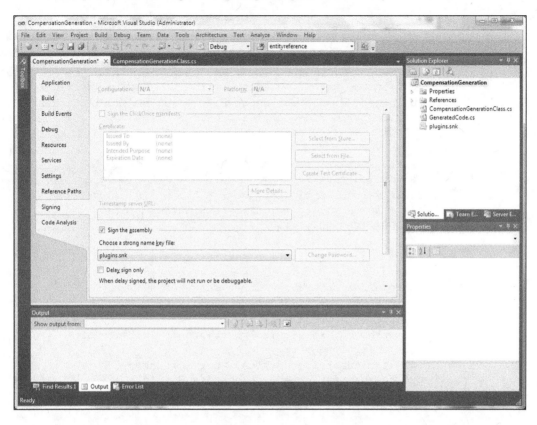

5. Run the `crmsvcutil.exe` command to generate strongly-typed classes for the entities in the ACM organization, for early binding:

```
\sdk\bin>crmsvcutil.exe /url:http://localhost:5555/ACM/
XRMServices/2011/Organization.svc /out:GeneratedCode.cs
```

6. Add `GeneratedCode.cs` into solution.

7. Create a new Class file called `QueryConnection.cs`. This does the query work in CRM, listing all flights and their crew members. See the following code:

```
using System;
usingSystem.Collections.Generic;
usingSystem.Linq;
usingSystem.Text;
usingSystem.ServiceModel;
usingMicrosoft.Xrm.Sdk;
usingMicrosoft.Xrm.Sdk.Client;
```

```
namespace CompensationGeneration
{

  public class CompensationGenerationClass: IPlugin
  {
    public void Execute(IServiceProviderserviceProvider)
    {
      // Obtain the execution context from the service provider.
      IPluginExecutionContext context = (IPluginExecutionContext)
        serviceProvider.GetService(typeof(
        IPluginExecutionContext));

      // Extract the tracing service for use in debugging
      // sandboxed plug-ins.
      ITracingServicetracingService =
        (ITracingService)serviceProvider.GetService(
        typeof(ITracingService));

      // Obtain the organization service reference.
      IOrganizationServiceFactoryserviceFactory =
        (IOrganizationServiceFactory)serviceProvider.
        GetService(typeof(IOrganizationServiceFactory));

      // Use the context service to create an instance of
         IOrganizationService.
      IOrganizationService service = serviceFactory.
        CreateOrganizationService(context.UserId);

      try
      {
        // The InputParameters collection contains all the data
           passed in the message request.
        if (context.InputParameters.Contains("Target") &&
        context.InputParameters["Target"] is Entity)
        {
          if (context.MessageName == "Create")
          {
            // Obtain the target entity from the input
               parmameters.
            Entity entity = (Entity)context.
              InputParameters["Target"];

            // Verify that the entity represents a connection.
            if (entity.LogicalName != "connection")
            return;
```

```
            //Gets the entity as the connection type.
            Connection connection = entity.ToEntity<Connection>();

            // If the connection record match the connection role,
                then create a new compensation.
            if (CheckConnectionRecords(service, connection))
            {
                CreateCompenstaion(service, connection);
            }
        }

        if (context.MessageName == "Update")
        {
            // Gets the properties of the primary entity before
                the core platform operation has begins.
            if (context.PreEntityImages.Contains(
                "ConnectionImage") && context.PreEntityImages[
                "ConnectionImage"] is Entity)
            {
                Entity entity = (Entity)context.PreEntityImages[
                    "ConnectionImage"];
                if (entity.LogicalName != "connection")
                return;

                Connection connection =
                    entity.ToEntity<Connection>();

                // If the old connection record match the connection
                    role, then delete the old compensation.
                if (CheckConnectionRecords(service, connection))
                {
                    DeleteCompensation(
                        service, context.PrimaryEntityId);
                }
            }

            // Gets the properties of the primary entity after the
                core platform operation has been completed.
            if (context.PostEntityImages.Contains(
                "ConnectionImage") && context.PostEntityImages[
                "ConnectionImage"] is Entity)
            {
                Entity entity = (Entity)context.PostEntityImages[
                    "ConnectionImage"];
                if (entity.LogicalName != "connection")
                return;
```

```
      Connection connection =
        entity.ToEntity<Connection>();

      // If the new connection record match the connection
          role, then create a new compensation.
      if (CheckConnectionRecords(service, connection))
      {
        CreateCompenstaion(service, connection);
      }
    }
  }
}

if (context.InputParameters.Contains("Target") &&
  context.InputParameters[
  "Target"] is EntityReference)
{
  if (context.MessageName == "Delete")
  {
    // Identifies a record. The EntityReference class
    replaces the Moniker class from Microsoft Dynamics
    CRM 4.0.
    EntityReference entity =
      (EntityReference)context.InputParameters["Target"];
    if (entity.LogicalName != "connection")
    return;

    using (varorgContext = new
      OrganizationServiceContext(service))
    {
      // Get the connection record that being deleted.
      Connection connection = orgContext.CreateQuery<
        Connection>().Where(
        c =>c.Id == entity.Id).First();

      // If the connection record match the connection
          role, then delete the existing compensation.
      if (CheckConnectionRecords(service, connection))
      {
        DeleteCompensation(
          service, context.PrimaryEntityId);
      }
    }
  }
}
```

```
      }

      catch (FaultException<OrganizationServiceFault> ex)
      {
        throw new InvalidPluginExecutionException(
          "An error occurred in the CompensationGeneration
          plug-in.", ex);
      }

      catch (Exception ex)
      {
        tracingService.Trace("CompensationGeneration: {0}",
          ex.ToString());
        throw;
      }
    }

    privateboolCheckConnectionRecords(
      IOrganizationService service, Connection connection)
    {
      // Validate the connection record.
      if (connection.Record1Id != null &&
        connection.Record1RoleId != null &&
        connection.Record2Id != null &&
        connection.Record2RoleId != null)
      {
        // Each connection will create two records on each side.
          We just need to stick on 1 side.
        if (connection.Record1Id.LogicalName == "contact"
          &&CheckConnectionRoleCategory(
          service, connection.Record1RoleId.Id)
          && connection.Record2Id.LogicalName == "acm_flight"
          &&CheckConnectionRoleCategory(
          service, connection.Record2RoleId.Id))
        {
          // Create a new compensation.
          return true;
        }
      }

      return false;
    }

    privateboolCheckConnectionRoleCategory(
      IOrganizationService service, GuidRoleID)
    {
```

```
        using (varorgContext = new
          OrganizationServiceContext(service))
        {
          varconnectionrole = from cr in
            orgContext.CreateQuery<ConnectionRole>()
            wherecr.ConnectionRoleId == RoleID
            wherecr.Category.Value == 100000000
            //Category="Flight Crew"
          selectcr;

          if (connectionrole.ToList().Count > 0)
          return true;
          else
          return false;
        }
      }

      private void CreateCompenstaion(IOrganizationService service,
        Connection connection)
      {
        using (varorgContext = new
          OrganizationServiceContext(service))
        {
          //Single query to get the crewmember record
          var crewmember = (from c in
            orgContext.CreateQuery<Contact>()
          wherec.ContactId == connection.Record1Id.Id
            select c).Single();

          Money HourlyDutyPay = new
            Money(crewmember.acm_HourlyDutyPay.Value);
          stringBaseCity = crewmember.Address1_City;
          stringBaseCountry = crewmember.Address1_Country;

          //Single query to get the flight record
          var flight = (from f in
            orgContext.CreateQuery<acm_flight>()
          wheref.acm_flightId == connection.Record2Id.Id
            select f).Single();

          intFlightTime = flight.acm_FlightTime.Value;
          intLayoverTime = flight.acm_LayoverTime.Value;
          OptionSetValueFlightType = new
            OptionSetValue(flight.acm_FlightType.Value);

          //Single query to get the airport record
```

```
var airport = (from fr in
  orgContext.CreateQuery<acm_flightroute>()
  join a in orgContext.CreateQuery<acm_airport>()
  on fr.acm_To.Id equals a.acm_airportId
  wherefr.acm_flightrouteId ==
  flight.acm_FlightRoute.Id
  select a).Single();

Money PerDiem = new Money(airport.acm_PerDiem.Value);
stringLayoverCity = airport.acm_City;
stringLayoverCountry = airport.acm_Country;

//Create compensation record
Entity compensation = new Entity("acm_compensation");
compensation["acm_crewmember"] = new
  EntityReference(connection.Record1Id.LogicalName,
  connection.Record1Id.Id);
compensation["acm_flight"] = new
  EntityReference(connection.Record2Id.LogicalName,
  connection.Record2Id.Id);

if (FlightTime> 0)
  compensation["acm_flighttime"] = FlightTime;

if (LayoverTime> 0)
  compensation["acm_layovertime"] = LayoverTime;

if (HourlyDutyPay != null)
  compensation["acm_hourlydutypay"] = HourlyDutyPay;

if (FlightType != null)
  compensation["acm_flighttype"] = FlightType;

if (PerDiem != null)
  compensation["acm_perdiem"] = PerDiem;

// Calculate total compensation
if (FlightTime> 0 &&LayoverTime> 0
  &&HourlyDutyPay != null &&FlightType != null
  &&PerDiem != null)
{
  Money Compensation;
  decimalOnDutyPay = HourlyDutyPay.Value *
    FlightTime / 60;
  decimalLayoverPay = PerDiem.Value * LayoverTime / 60;
```

```
            if (FlightType.Value != 1)
            {
              OnDutyPay = OnDutyPay * 2;
            }
            if (BaseCity == LayoverCity&&BaseCountry ==
              LayoverCountry)
            {
              Compensation = new Money(OnDutyPay);
            }
            else
            {
              Compensation = new Money(OnDutyPay + LayoverPay);
            }

            compensation["acm_compensation"] = Compensation;
            compensation["subject"] = "Compensation created for: " +
              crewmember.FullName + " on " + flight.acm_name + "
              by " + connection.Id.ToString();

          }
          service.Create(compensation);
        }
      }

    private void DeleteCompensation(
      IOrganizationService service, GuidConnectionID)
    {
      using (varorgContext = new
        OrganizationServiceContext(service))
      {
        var compensations = from c in
          orgContext.CreateQuery<acm_compensation>()
          wherec.Subject.Contains(ConnectionID.ToString())
          select c;

        foreach (acm_compensation compensation in compensations)
        {
          service.Delete(acm_compensation.EntityLogicalName,
            compensation.Id);
        }
      }
    }

  }
}
```

8. Register the Plug-in:

   a. Run the Plug-in Registration Tool (this can be found in the CRM 2011 SDK folder: `sdk\tools\pluginregistration\bin\Debug\PluginRegistration.exe`)

   b. Click the **Create New Connection** button on the toolbar, provide the connection information, and then click on **Connect**.

      The discovery URLs for the worldwide Microsoft Dynamics CRM Online data centers are:

      * North America: `https://dev.crm.dynamics.com`
      * EMEA: `https://dev.crm4.dynamics.com`
      * APAC: `https://dev.crm5.dynamics.com`

   c. Once connected, go to **Register | Register New Plugin**, and then select the Plug-in DLL file you just built. Select the **Sandbox** as the isolation mode and **Database** as the assembly location, and then click the **Register selected Plugins** button.

   d. Now that the Plug-in assembly has been registered, we need to register three steps for connections: Create, Delete, and Update message. Right-click on the **CompensationGeneration** assembly, and select **Register New Step**. The first step is as follows:

CompensationGeneration Plug-in Steps			
Message	Create	Delete	Update
Primary Entity	connection	connection	connection
Filtering Attributes	All	All	record1id, record2id, record1roleid, record2roleid
Run in User's Context	Calling User	Calling User	Calling User
Eventing Pipeline	Post-operation	Pre-operation	Post-operation
Execution Mode	Synchronous	Synchronous	Synchronous
Deployment	Server	Server	Server

   e. On the Update step, we also need to register an Image to get the primary entity before and after the core platform operation begins. Right-click on the **Update** step, select **Register New Image**, and fill in the following information:

      * Image Type: Pre Image, Post Image
      * Name/Entity Alias: ConnectionImage

- Parameters: record1id, record2id, record1roleid, record2roleid

f. A completed Plug-in registration should look like the example shown in the following screenshot:

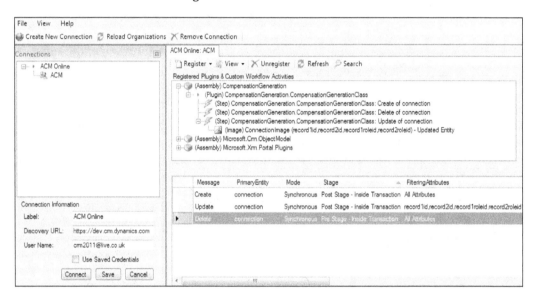

Using the CRM Developer Toolkit to build a Plug-in

It's also recommended to use the CRM Developer Toolkit when building a Plug-in. The Developer's Toolkit for Microsoft Dynamics CRM 2011 is a set of Visual Studio integration tools focused on accelerating the development of custom code for Dynamics CRM 2011. The Toolkit supports the end-to-end creation and deployment of CRM Plug-ins, custom workflows, Silverlight applications, and other Web resources, including JavaScript and HTML. Dynamics CRM developers can write all of their custom code from within Visual Studio, using native tools and build processes, and then automatically deploy them to the CRM Server.

Processes

In Microsoft Dynamics CRM 2011, Workflows and Dialogs are called Processes.

- Workflow: An automated asynchronous process that is triggered by CRM events, or an asynchronous process that is initially triggered by user input, and then runs in the background to completion without interacting with the user.

- Dialog: A synchronous process that requires the user's input via a wizard-like web interface from the beginning to completion.

A detailed comparison of Workflows and Dialogs is available in the SDK, at: `http://msdn.microsoft.com/en-us/library/gg309471.aspx`. A summary is provided below.

Workflows	Dialogs
Can either be started by a user or be automated.	Must be started by a user.
Are asynchronous processes, and do not require user input to run to completion. These processes run in the background.	Are synchronous processes, and require user input to run to completion. When you run these processes, a wizard-like interface is presented to you so that you can make appropriate selections to run the processes.
The entity that stores the details about a running workflow is `AsyncOperation`.	The entity that stores information generated by a running dialog is the `ProcessSession` (dialog session) entity.
Both Windows Workflow Foundation 4 and Windows Workflow Foundation 3.5 custom activities are supported.	Only Windows Workflow Foundation 4 custom activities are supported.
Triggers are supported for workflows. For a list of supported triggers, see *Supported Types, Triggers, and Entities for Processes (Workflows and Dialogs)*, at: `http://msdn.microsoft.com/en-us/library/gg328562.aspx`.	Triggers are not supported for dialogs.
Workflows that are created or updated outside of Microsoft Dynamics CRM, by creating or updating the underlying XAML file, are supported in Microsoft Dynamics CRM. For information about these custom XAML workflows, see *Custom XAML Workflows*, at: `http://msdn.microsoft.com/en-us/library/gg309458.aspx`.	Dialogs that are created or updated outside of Microsoft Dynamics CRM, by creating or updating the underlying XAML file, are not supported in Microsoft Dynamics CRM.

Workflow

Workflows are automated business processes that consist of Steps and Actions. A Workflow is an asynchronous processes; it doesn't require user input data. A Workflow can be triggered by an event (automated Workflow) or by a user (manual Workflow).

 Microsoft Dynamics CRM 2011 On-premises also supports custom Workflow Activities (like CRM 4.0) and custom XAML Workflows. An XAML Workflow can be visually designed and created in Visual Studio Workflow Designer, without coding.

Workflow versus Plug-ins

There are some major differences between Workflows and Plug-ins:

- Workflows run asynchronously in the background. Plug-ins can run both asynchronously and synchronously.

- Workflows can be triggered manually (security context of the user who trigged it), or automatically (security context of the workflow owner) by selected events. Plug-ins can only be trigged by the message (security context of the CRM Web application pool identity) for which they're registered.

- Workflows provide the flexibility to allow admin users to change the business process without changing the code in Visual Studio. Plug-ins have to be recompiled by developers, using Visual Studio.

- Workflows don't execute offline. Plug-ins support both online and offline execution.

- Workflows don't support impersonation. Plug-ins do support impersonation.

- Workflows can be paused, postponed, cancelled, and resumed. The workflow state is automatically saved before it is paused or postponed. Plug-ins execute to completion; the execution is required to complete its execution within a two minute time limit.

- Workflows can be developed through the CRM Workflow web application, Visual Studio Workflow Designer (Custom XAML Workflows (on-premises only)) or Visual Studio (Custom Workflow Activities (on-premises only)). Plug-ins can only be developed through Visual Studio.

Workflows are based on the Windows Workflow Foundation 4. This uses the same event mode for Plug-ins. However, the pre-event doesn't support asynchronous processes. Choose Workflows when you require flexibility and user involvement. Choose Plug-ins when you require immediate platform response impersonation or "Pre-" events. Also bear in mind that Microsoft Dynamics CRM 2011 Online only supports the Sandbox Plug-ins and Workflows that are customized via the CRM Workflow web application (non-Custom Workflows).

A Workflow example

You might have noticed that the flight name is empty! We can simply generate the flight name from the Flight Number and Departure Time.

1. Open the CRM web application, go to the **ACM solution** | **Processes**, and create a new process with the following information:

   - Process name: Update Flight Name
   - Entity: Flight
   - Category: Workflow
   - Type: New blank process

2. Set up the Process properties as follows:

   - Process name: Update Flight Name
   - Activate As: Process
   - Scope: Organization
   - Start When:
     - Record is created
     - Record fields change (Flight Route, Departure Time)

3. Add one step (**Update Record | Flight**), and then set the properties of the flight record:

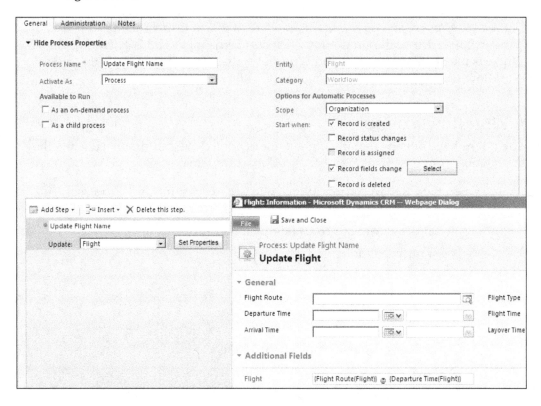

4. Save and activate the Workflow.

That's it. Now go ahead and add a new flight record (or update the on Flight Route or Departure Time for an existing Flight record); you will see that the Flight name is generated by the CRM workflow (after a few seconds). You can check the Workflow processes by clicking the **Processes** link in the workflow window.Alternatively, you can go to **Settings | System Jobs** in order to monitor a Workflow process.

In this example, we can see that the Workflow process is a system job (asynchronous operation) that is running in the background. The job owner (the running credential of this process) for the automatic Workflow is the Workflow owner (in our case). For the on-demand Workflow, the running credential is the user who triggers the process.

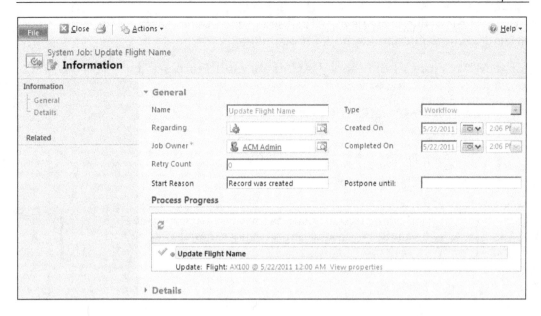

Dialog

Dialogs are the interactive and synchronous processes that collect and process information by using wizard-like web interfaces to direct users through a process.

Dialogs require user's input to run the processes. A dialog can only be run online through the CRM Web application; you cannot run a dialog using CRM SDK or CRM Outlook Offline Access.

A Dialog example

Let's start building a Dialog to understand how it works. In this demo, we are going to build a Dialog to help ACM operators to quickly add comments to an existing Flight. A Phonecall record will be created after the Dialog process.

So the user story is like this: A crewmember calls in >>an ACM operator answers the phone and finds out the reason of the call >> verifies the caller's identity >> the crew member makes a comment about a flight >> the ACM operator carries out the request >> a Phonecall record is created in the CRM, with the sender (Crew Member) and related (Flight) information.

We can use a Dialog to create the structured process outlined above, and offer a wizard-like web interface to the ACM operators.

Go to **ACM Settings | Solutions | ACMSolution | Processes**, and click **New**, in order to create a Dialog process:

- Process name: Add Activity to Flight
- Entity: User
- Category: Dialog
- Type: New blank process

 Notice that this Dialog doesn't have to apply to the Flight entity. We choose the User entity to host the Dialog for later use.

The steps are as follows:

1. Page: Prompt and Response:
    - Statement Label: Ask for employee ID
    - Prompt Text: Hello, can I have your employee ID please?
    - Response Type: Single Line

2. Query CRM Data:
    - Statement Label: Query crewmembers via the employee ID
    - Look for: "Crew Members" "Employee" "Equals" " x"
    - Then go to the Modify Query Variables, change the Variable1 to the {Response Text (Ask for employee id)}

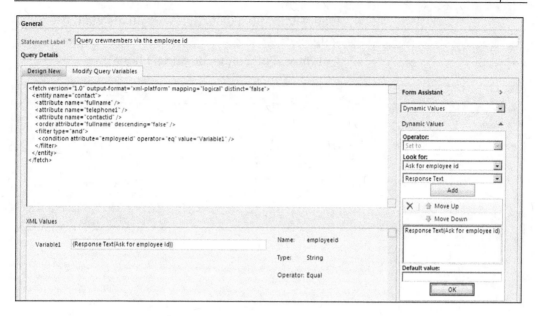

3. Check condition:

- If "Query crewmembers via the employee id" "Records" "Is Greater Than or Equal to" "1", Then:

  3.1 Page: Prompt and Response:

  - Statement Label: Verify caller's identity
  - Prompt Text: Can you confirm your fullname and business phone number please?
  - Response Type: Option (picklist)
  - Provide Values: Query CRM data

- Query Variables: Query crewmembers via the employee ID
- Columns: Full Name, Business Phone

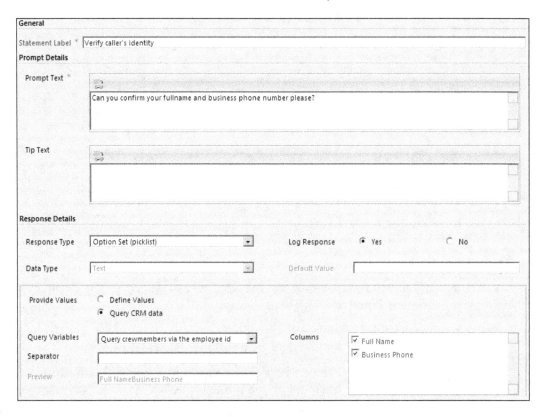

3.2 Page: Prompt and Response:
- Statement Label: Ask for flight number
- Prompt Text: What is the flight number?
- Response Type: Single Line

3.3 Query CRM Data:
- Statement Label: Query flight via flight name
- Look for: "Flights" "Flight Name" "Begins With" " x"
- Then go to the Modify Query Variables, change the Variable1 to: {Response Text(Ask for flight number)}

3.4 Check Condition:

- If "Query flight via flight name" "Records" "Is Greater Than or Equal to" "1", Then:

  3.4.1 Page: Prompt and Response:

  - Statement Label: Confirm the flight
  - Prompt Text: Please confirm the flight.
  - Response Type: Option (picklist)
  - Provide Values: Query CRM data
  - Query Variables: Query flight via flight name
  - Columns: Flight Name, Created On

  3.4.2 Page: Prompt and Response:

  - Statement Label: Get the comment of this flight
  - Prompt Text: What is it about this flight?
  - Response Type: Multiple Lines (Text Only)

  3.4.3 Create Record: Phone Call

  - Sender: {Contact(Verify caller's identity (Crew Member))}
  - Phone Number: {Business Phone(Verify caller's identity (Crew Member))}
  - Direction: Incoming
  - Subject: {Full Name(Verify caller's identity (Crew Member))} made a comment on {Flight Name(Confirm the flight (Flight))}
  - Description: {Response Text(Get the comment of this flight)}
  - Regarding: {Flight(Confirm the flight (Flight))}
  - Due: {Execution Time(Process)}
  - Category: Comments

4. Stop Dialog.

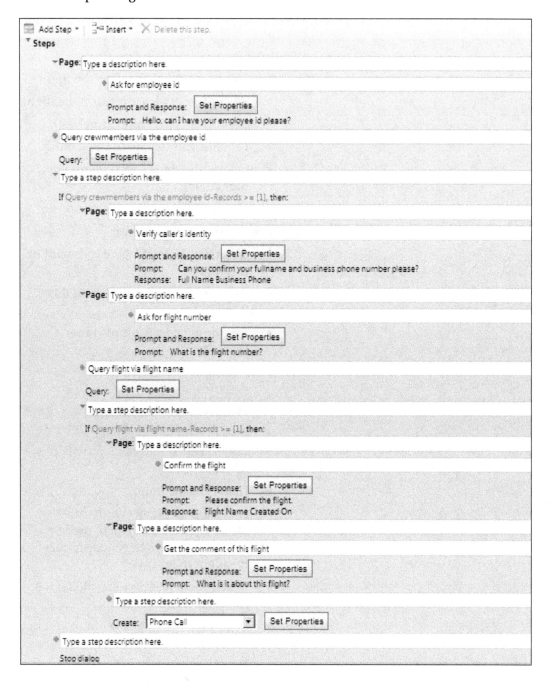

OK, the Dialog has been created. Make sure that you select both "as on-demand process" and "as child process", then save and activate the Dialog. Now we need to create a parent Dialog, "Call Center Dialog", that can direct the ACM operators to the correct category (that is, Add Activity to Flight).

The steps are as follows:

1. Page: Prompt and Response:
    - Statement Label: Phone call category
    - Prompt Text: Hello, what can I do for you?
    - Tip Text: Define the phone call category.
    - Response Type: Option Set
    - Provide Values: Define Values
    - Response Values:
        ◦ Value: 0
        ◦ Label: Adding comments to a flight

2. Check Condition:
    - If "Phone call category" "Response Value" "Equals" "0", Then
        2.1 Link Child Dialog
            - User: Add Activity to Flight

3. Stop Dialog.

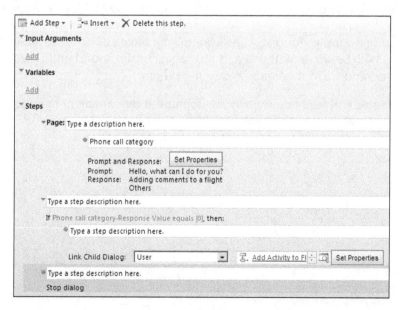

Now, you can test the Dialog by going to **ACM Settings | Administration | Users**, then selecting the system user, and clicking the **Start Dialog** on the ribbon bar. Then run the "Call Center Dialog".

You can also start the Dialog by using a URL: `http://CRMServer_Name/Org_Name/cs/dialog/rundialog.aspx?DialogId=DialogID&EntityName=EntityLogicalName&ObjectId=EntityObjectId`.

In the URL, we can fix the `EntityName` to "systemuser" and the `ObjectId` to a CRM system administrator account which always exists. So we can then add a button on the ribbon bar of the CRM main form, and call the Dialog directly, using the URL, by clicking the button on the ribbon.

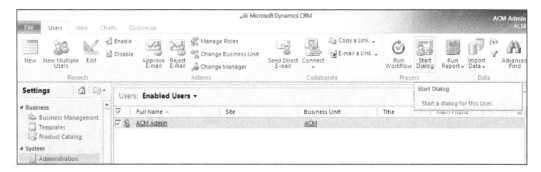

Summary

In this chapter, we introduced the Microsoft Dynamics CRM 2011 Plug-ins and Processes (Workflows and Dialogs), compared the differences between them, and saw some code examples for our ACM system. We have also introduced the Event Framework, Web Services methods and messages, Early-Bound and Late-Bound Entity Classes, and CRM data queries, among others.

The next chapter will focus on improving document management in your CRM system, by integrating it with SharePoint 2010.

6
SharePoint Integration

Microsoft Dynamics CRM 2011 supports SharePoint 2007/2010 integration to improve document management in CRM. The previous versions of CRM didn't have a solid out-of-the-box solution for document management except 'Notes' and 'Articles'. The SharePoint integration feature provides the same look and feel inside CRM. Users can operate documents inside CRM just like in SharePoint. SharePoint 2010 is recommended, because documents from SharePoint 2007 are displayed in an IFRAME, and folders cannot be automatically created on the SharePoint server.

This task will show you how to enable and configure the SharePoint integration feature in Microsoft Dynamics CRM 2011.

Preparing for SharePoint integration

The airline company is using Microsoft SharePoint 2010 internally. They like the document management capability in SharePoint, as they have some experience in CRM. They especially want to have documents relating to Airport, Crew Member, and Flight.

SharePoint site collection

First of all, we need to create a SharePoint 2010 site collection to host the CRM documents for Airport, Crew Member, and Flight.

Go to the SharePoint 2010 central administration site, create a new web application, and then create a new site collection called CRM Documents. Select the "Document Center" as the template when creating the site collection. The URL for the site collection is `http://bps:6666`.

If you have installed SharePoint Foundation 2010, you can also create a site collection in it.

The following screenshot shows the homepage of the CRM Documents.

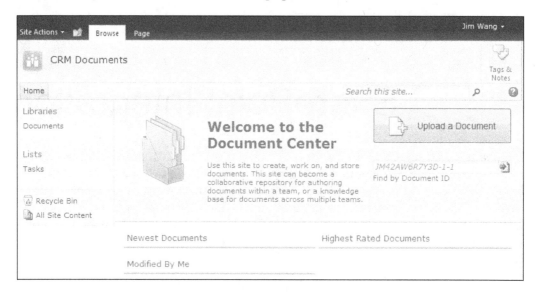

Next, we will need to install the CRM List Component on this SharePoint site collection.

CRM List Component for SharePoint

The Microsoft Dynamics CRM 2011 List component for SharePoint makes the CRM documents that are stored on SharePoint available in a format that has the look and feel of Microsoft Dynamics CRM. This component also allows Microsoft Dynamics CRM to automatically create folders that will be used to store documents related to CRM records on SharePoint. The CRM List Component is a SharePoint sandbox solution package file (.wsp) that can be installed on SharePoint 2010 Server and SharePoint 2010 Online. It provides two handy features for CRM/SharePoint integration:

1. SharePoint integration in CRM grid (same look and feel).
2. Automatic folder (document locations) creation on SharePoint.

 Note: The List Component supports SharePoint 2010 only; SharePoint 2007 will be integrated with CRM through the use of iFrames. There is no folder auto-creation function for a non-CRM List Component environment.

To install CRM List Component on SharePoint server, we need to make sure that the "Microsoft SharePoint User Code Host" service, which allows the execution of user code in a sandbox solution, is started. Then, install the solution package (.wsp) on the SharePoint site collection. Browse to the SharePoint site collection, click the **Site Settings** link, click on **Solutions**, and then select **Upload Solution** from the **Solutions** ribbon. Next, navigate to and upload the CRM List Component WSP file, and then activate it.

The following screenshot shows the CRM List Component in SharePoint 2010 Solutions (Go to **CRM Documents site collection | Site Settings | Solutions**):

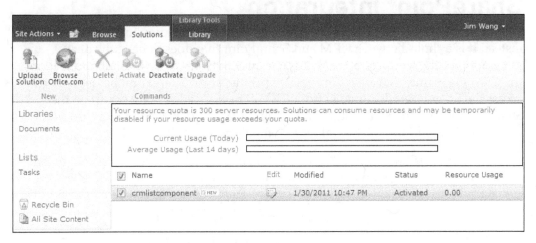

Notice that, for the on-premise SharePoint deployment, you may have to add the .htc extension to the list of the allowed file types. Document Management is responsible for button actions through Microsoft Dynamics CRM. You can do this through the SharePoint Management Console or Windows PowerShell. Type in: .\ AllowHtcExtn.ps1 <Web Application URL>, for example:

```
.\AllowHtcExtn.ps1 http://bps:6666
```

This PowerShell command will turn on the Microsoft SharePoint Foundation User Code Service, and add HTC extensions to the list of allowed extensions.

You may reference the "Microsoft Dynamics CRM List Component for Microsoft SharePoint Server 2010 Readme" for more information on the CRM List Component.

 Note: The current version (05.00.9688.583) of CRM List Component for SharePoint doesn't support Office365 | SharePoint Online. The on-line version of the list component will be released in a future version.

SharePoint Integration

The out-of-the-box integration is not a functional, fully-bonding implementation, instead it is a "link" between CRM and SharePoint that doesn't have the deep integration of the two products. That is, because they are two different applications, the CRM users must have the appropriate privileges on SharePoint before they can access the SharePoint documents from CRM. These privileges are set up on the SharePoint side, and not through CRM. The CRM Outlook client doesn't provide document integration with SharePoint when it's in the Offline mode.

Nevertheless, the SharePoint integration still enhances the document management ability in Microsoft Dynamics CRM. The following diagram shows how it works:

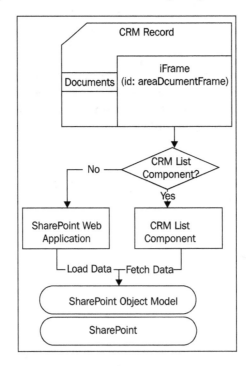

Document Management Settings

To enable the SharePoint integrated document management feature in CRM, open the Microsoft Dynamics CRM homepage, and go to **Settings | Document Management | Document Management Settings**.

In our ACM system, we want to enable the document management feature for Airport, Flight, and Crew Members, in order to manage the related documents for various purposes. So select these three entities, and type in a valid SharePoint site URL (it can be either a site collection or a site), then click **Next**.

There are two types of folder structures:

1. Based on an account/contact entity; the folder structure is as follows: `<DefaultSite>/Accounts/<accountname>/<EntityName>/<recordna me>`, for example: `http://SPServer/Accounts/account1/Opportunity/opportunty1`.

2. Based on an independent entity; the folder structure is as follows: `<DefaultSite>/<EntityName>/<recordname>`, for example: `http://SPServer/Opportunity/opportunty1`.

In our case, we choose the independent folder structure. Because the ACM records don't have the strict hierarchy, it makes more sense to choose the independent entity. So deselect the "Based on entity" option, and then click **Next**.

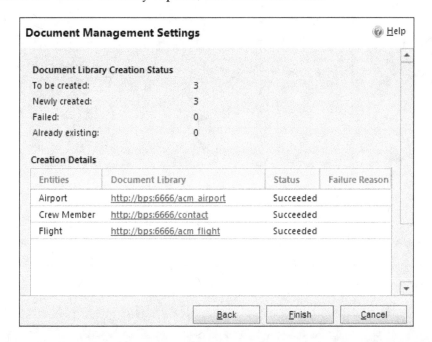

Once the **Document Library Creation Status** dialog box indicates that CRM has created three document libraries for each entity in the SharePoint site collection "CRM Documents" we just created, click on **Finish**.

You may notice that the name of Document Library uses the Display Name of the CRM entity, whereas the URL uses the schema name.

When opening a CRM entity that has the document management feature enabled, a link called **Documents** will appear in the left-hand navigation bar of this entity. Click on this link, and CRM will create a new folder in SharePoint using the entity's primary attribute (by default) of this record. You can change the folder name and location later on.

For example, go to **Workplace | Crew Members**, and open the record Grace Allen. Because the document management feature has been enabled for Crew Members, we can see a link in the left-hand navigation panel called **Documents**. By clicking the link CRM will create a folder in SharePoint (under the Crew Members document library) called Grace Allen (using the "fullname" value, which is the primary field of Crew Member).

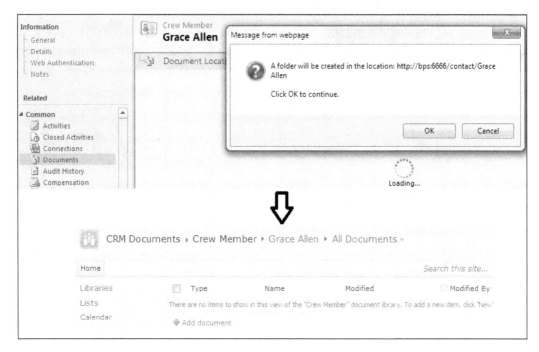

SharePoint Sites and Document Locations

During the Document Management Settings progress, CRM creates a default SharePoint site. We can see it from **Settings** | **Document Management** | **SharePoint Sites**.

Although it's possible to set up multiple site collections per CRM tenant, you should carefully choose the site structure and make it fit in your organization's security hierarchies. For example, you could have one site collection per CRM entity for the security and governance reasons. Or just use one site collection per CRM tenant on a permissive environment.

For testing purposes, let's go ahead and create another site under the default site collection. First of all, we need to create a site from SharePoint—that is, a "Records Center" site. Go to the SharePoint web application, click the **Site Actions** button, and then select **New Site**. In the site template, select **Records Center**. **Title** and **URL** are both **Records Center**.

So now we have a site collection: `http://bps:6666/` and a site: `http://bps:6666/Records Center/`.

Back in CRM, go to **Settings** | **Document Management** | **SharePoint Sites**, and create a new SharePoint Site with the information shown in the following screenshot. Don't forget to click the **Validate** button to validate the site we just saved:

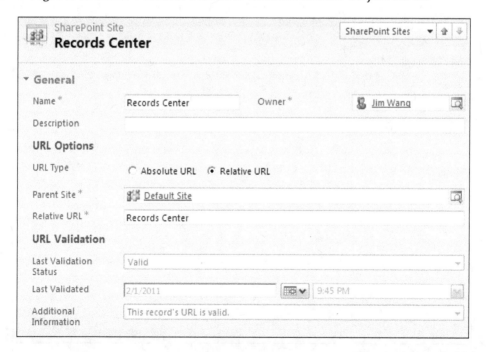

As we see here, we are using a relative URL for the new **Records Center** site.

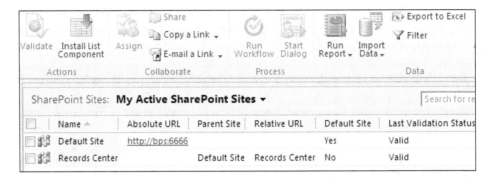

Now that we have two SharePoint Sites in CRM, let's open another Crew Member record and do something different. Go to **Workplace | Crew Members**, open the record **Sue Ellis**, and click the **Documents** link in the left-hand navigation bar. Because this record doesn't have a SharePoint location (folder) associated with it, CRM will ask you to create a new folder in the default location (`http://bps:6666/ contact`). At this stage, we choose **Cancel**. Now click the **Add Location** button on the ribbon bar, choose the **Create a new folder** option, and then select the **Records Center** site as the parent site, keep the folder name as **Sue Ellis**, and click **Save**. CRM will create a folder for this record under the **Records Center** site. Click **OK** to continue:

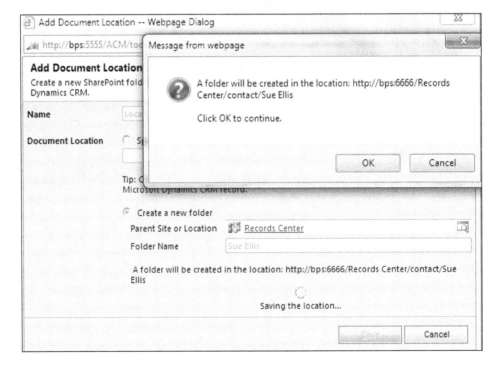

If we now browse to **Settings | Document Management | SharePoint Document Locations**, we will see that four locations have been created so far; notice that Grace Allen and Sue Ellis are using different sites:

	Name ▲	Regarding	Absolute URL	Parent Site or Location	Relative URL	
	Documents on Default Site 1			Default Site	contact	
	Documents on Default Site 1	Grace Allen		Documents on Default Site 1	Grace Allen	
	Location 1			Records Center	contact	
	Location 1	Sue Ellis		Location 1	Sue Ellis	

Document Locations: **Active Document Locations ▾**

The hierarchy of the SharePoint Sites and Document Locations can be visualized as shown in the next screenshot. As you can see, both a SharePoint site collection and a site can host entities (document library). A CRM record can be associated with multiple locations that host documents.

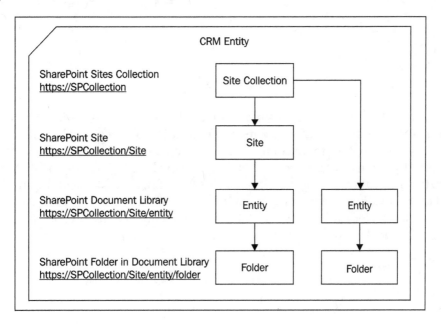

There is a potential need that a CRM record could be associated with many document locations, which will ultimately make it unmanageable. CRM has a simple, manual solution for that: you can not only add locations, but can also edit locations for the current view:

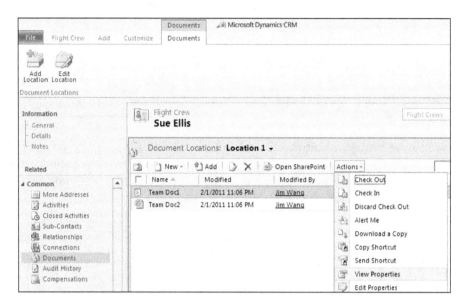

Go ahead and click the **Edit Location** button on the ribbon bar. Change the **Parent Site or Location** lookup to **Documents on Default Site 1** (the site collection); CRM will create another folder in the site collection. Notice that CRM doesn't automatically bring our test documents into the new location. As we mentioned earlier, the integration is a "link" between CRM and SharePoint; CRM doesn't operate SharePoint fully. So in such a case, we will have to move the documents from the old location to a new location in SharePoint. This can be done manually, or by a program via custom code development in SharePoint.

Edit Document Location
Create a new SharePoint folder or add an existing SharePoint folder as a document location in Microsoft Dynamics CRM.

Name	Documents on Default Site 1

Document Location ○ Specify the URL of an existing SharePoint folder

Tip: Copy the URL of the existing SharePoint folder here to associate the folder with this Microsoft Dynamics CRM record.

● Specify the name of an existing folder or create a new folder

Parent Site or Location   Documents on Default Site 1

Folder Name   Sue Ellis

Following example shows how to programmatically list all entities that have document management enabled; as well as list the record's ID and the absolute URL of SharePoint Document Location.

 More detail about the Microsoft Dynamics CRM 2011 server-side programming will be introduced in *Chapter 5, Server-Side Programming*.

```
/*
 * List All Entities That Have Document Management Enabled.
 * List Record's ID and the Absolute URL of the SharePoint Document
   Location.
 *
 * */

using System;
using System.Collections.Generic;
using System.Linq;
using System.Text;
using System.ServiceModel.Description;
using System.Net;
using Microsoft.Xrm.Sdk.Client;
using Microsoft.Xrm.Sdk;
using Microsoft.Xrm.Sdk.Messages;
using Microsoft.Xrm.Sdk.Metadata;
using Microsoft.Xrm.Sdk.Query;
using Microsoft.Crm.Sdk.Messages;

namespace CRMSharePointQuery
{
  class Program
  {
    static void Main(string[] args)
    {
      Uri OrganizationUri = new
                          Uri("http://bps:5555/ACM/XRMServices/2011
                          /Organization.svc");
      Uri HomeRealmUri = null;
      ClientCredentials Credentials = new ClientCredentials();
      Credentials.Windows.ClientCredential =
                          CredentialCache.DefaultNetworkCredentials;

      try
      {
```

```
        //Initializes a new instance of the CRM
          OrganizationServiceProxy class.
        using (OrganizationServiceProxy serviceProxy =
               new OrganizationServiceProxy(OrganizationUri,
               HomeRealmUri, Credentials, null))
        {
          //This statement is required to enable early-bound type
            support.
          serviceProxy.EnableProxyTypes();
          IOrganizationService service =
                            (IOrganizationService)serviceProxy;

          //Create the OrganizationServiceContext object that will
            generate the IQueryable collections for LINQ calls.
          OrganizationServiceContext context = new
                    OrganizationServiceContext(service);

          RetrieveAllEntitiesRequest request = new
                                    RetrieveAllEntitiesRequest
          {
            EntityFilters = EntityFilters.Entity,
            RetrieveAsIfPublished = true
          };

          //Retrieve the MetaData.
          RetrieveAllEntitiesResponse response =
               (RetrieveAllEntitiesResponse)service.Execute(request);

          foreach (EntityMetadata meta in response.EntityMetadata)
          {
            //If Document Management is enabled for this entity.
            if (meta.IsDocumentManagementEnabled.Value)
            {
              Console.WriteLine("========== Entity that has document
                                management enabled ==========");
              Console.WriteLine(meta.LogicalName);
              Console.WriteLine("---------- Record Id and Absolute
                                URL ----------");
              ListRecordIdAndAbsoluteURL(service, meta);
            }
          }
        }
      }
      catch (Exception ex)
```

```
        {
          errorHandler(ex);
        }

      Console.ReadLine();
    }


    //Display Errors.
    private static void errorHandler(Exception ex)
    {
      Console.WriteLine(ex.Message + ex.InnerException);
      //Console.ReadLine();
    }


    //List the Absolute URL of the SharePoint Location.
    private static void
            ListRecordIdAndAbsoluteURL(IOrganizationService service,
                                    EntityMetadata meta)
    {
      //Create Query Expression.
      QueryExpression query = new QueryExpression
      {
        EntityName = SharePointDocumentLocation.EntityLogicalName,
        LinkEntities =
        {
          new LinkEntity
          {
            LinkFromEntityName =
                SharePointDocumentLocation.EntityLogicalName,
            LinkFromAttributeName = "regardingobjectid",
            LinkToEntityName = meta.LogicalName,
            LinkToAttributeName = meta.PrimaryIdAttribute,
            Columns = new ColumnSet(meta.PrimaryIdAttribute),
            EntityAlias = "thisEntity",
            JoinOperator = JoinOperator.Inner,
          }
        }
      };

      EntityCollection ec = service.RetrieveMultiple(query);
      foreach (SharePointDocumentLocation spDocLoc in ec.Entities)
      {
        //Retrieve the absolute URL and the Site Collection URL of
          the SharePoint document location record.
```

```
RetrieveAbsoluteAndSiteCollectionUrlRequest retrieveRequest =
        new RetrieveAbsoluteAndSiteCollectionUrlRequest
{
  Target = new
           EntityReference(SharePointDocumentLocation.
           EntityLogicalName, spDocLoc.Id)
};

RetrieveAbsoluteAndSiteCollectionUrlResponse retrieveResponse
        = (RetrieveAbsoluteAndSiteCollectionUrlResponse)
           service.Execute(retrieveRequest);

Console.WriteLine("\r Record ID: " +
                  ((AliasedValue)spDocLoc["thisEntity." +
                  meta.PrimaryIdAttribute]).Value.ToString());
Console.WriteLine("\r SharePoint Document Location URL: " +
                  retrieveResponse.AbsoluteUrl);
Console.WriteLine("\r");
      }
    }
  }
}
```

SharePoint Document Set

In addition to using Folders to host CRM documents, it is also possible to use a Document Set to host CRM documents. Document Sets are a new feature introduced in SharePoint 2010 (not in SharePoint foundation). The same as Folder, Document Set is a SharePoint content type that manages a single deliverable entity that can include multiple documents or files. A Document Set also has a Document ID, so you can open a Document Set via `DocIdRedir.aspx`. Be aware of the following limitations of Document Sets:

- A Document Set can only host documents from one document library
- A Document Set can't contain Folders or other Documents Sets

For more information of Document Sets, please refer to *Document Sets Planning (SharePoint Server 2010)* on-line, at: `http://technet.microsoft.com/en-us/library/ff603637.aspx`.

It makes sense to host all individual relevant documents of a CRM record in a single Folder or Document Set. Doing so makes the management easier.

SharePoint Document ID

If we go to Sue Ellis's documents in CRM and upload two test documents, select one, and then click **Actions | View Properties**, we see the **Document ID** property. This is a new feature of SharePoint 2010, which can be used to easily locate the document in a site collection by using the following URL: `http://<sitecollectionurl>/_layouts/DocIdRedir.aspx?ID=`.

So in our case, we can open the selected test document via: `http://BPS:6666/_layouts/DocIdRedir.aspx?ID=JM42AW6R7Y3D-4-3`.

This feature is especially useful when trying to locate a document in a site collection.

Document View

The Document View doesn't come from CRM, it comes from SharePoint: the document library's default view. This means that you can add or remove columns in the default view of a document library in SharePoint:

Notice in the previous screenshot that we added **Document ID** and **Rating** to the document library default view. These columns are listed in CRM as well. Furthermore, we added a new content type: **Document Set**; this also shows in the **New** drop-down list.

Security settings

As we mentioned earlier, the CRM document integration isn't a fully-bonding integration with SharePoint. In addition to CRM security configuration, we will have to set up SharePoint security.

For the ACM system, all CRM users can be added to the default Contributors group in the SharePoint site, so that users are able to view, add, update, and delete list items and documents.

For more information of SharePoint security, please refer to: *Security and protection for SharePoint Server 2010* on-line, at `http://technet.microsoft.com/en-us/library/cc263215.aspx`.

Summary

In this chapter, we introduced the Microsoft Dynamics CRM 2011 Document Management features, including CRM List Components for SharePoint, Document Management Settings, SharePoint Sites, Document Locations, Document View, and Security settings.

We have also introduced some new features of SharePoint 2010 that can be used in CRM Document Management: Document ID and Document Set, which give you an idea when setting up the SharePoint site.

7
Charts and Dashboards

At this point of the book, we know how to input data into Microsoft Dynamics CRM. Now it's time to learn the new capabilities for analyzing our data and also for extracting data out of the system. Microsoft Dynamics CRM 2011 still has out-of-the-box reports for the sales module, marketing module, service module, and administration. However in this version, it introduces filters, charts and dashboards for us to better visualize our data in the system. In this chapter, we are going to cover these new business intelligence features such as filters, charts, and dashboards.

- What's new in CRM 2011?
- Working with Filters
- Working with Charts
- Reports

What is new in CRM 2011?

Microsoft Dynamics CRM 2011 offers different ways to look at the data in the system. Let's take a look at the history of how we perform analysis with our CRM data, as indicated in the following figure:

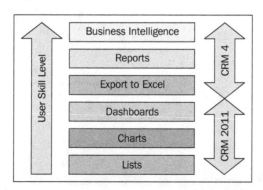

In the previous version of Microsoft CRM, we could export the data into an Excel document and then further slice and dice the data to perform analysis on the data. At the more advanced level, users could leverage the out-of-the-box reports or create their own reports to get the information to help them drive their business decisions, or for communicating performance to other people. The reports only represent a snapshot of the transaction data in time and do not provide any trend analysis or any real-time, continuous flow of business decisions the way that most business intelligence software does. Companies usually spend quite a bit of money to incorporate charts and dashboards or any other kind of business intelligence into their system. All of the ways mentioned require extra effort from the end users or may require developers.

Microsoft Dynamics CRM 2011 offers new ways for the end users to look at their data in their CRM system. It provides the filter functionality, which can be used at the list level on all out-of-the-box entities and also on custom entities. It also provides charts that we can use in conjunction with the views and filtered lists. Even better, Microsoft Dynamics CRM 2011 provides dashboard capability out-of-the-box and we can include charts, views, Iframes, reports, and custom web resources in the dashboard. All of these components are baked into the application. This increases the WOW factor for most people, gives the end users quick, actionable insights into the data, empowers users to create their own charts and dashboard, allows them to share or keep them private through the built-in security, and gives them a 30,000 feet view of the data, with drill-down capabilities.

Working with Filters

In the previous version of Microsoft Dynamics CRM, we had to export the data to Excel in order to perform filtering on the data. However, Microsoft Dynamics CRM 2011 gives end users the ability to filter on the list of data within the application. In this way, the users can obtain their important data in just a few clicks. To apply a filter to a list, simply click on the **Filter** button in the **Data** group on the ribbon:

You can also click the **Filter** button under the **View** tab on the ribbon. Here, we are going to apply a filter to the list and create our own custom filter.

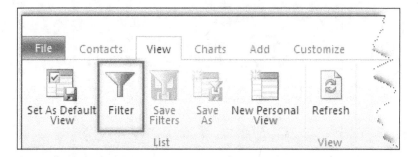

Applying Filters

Once we click on the filter button in the **Data** group on the ribbon, the filter arrows appear in the grid column headers as shown in the following screenshot:

Click on the arrow to the right of a column header to bring up the filter menu for that column, as shown in the next screenshot. The menu options change based on the attribute type. All attributes provide the capability to sort the data and also to check whether the attribute contains data:

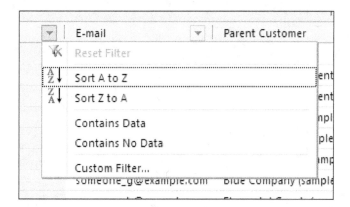

DateTime attributes contain extra filters to filter by day, week, month, year, fiscal period, and fiscal year, as shown in the following screenshot:

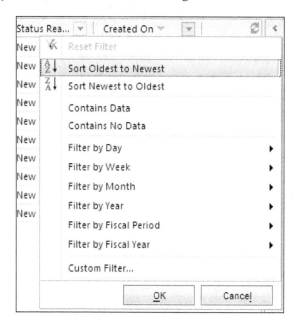

OptionSet attributes contain filters to filter by the list of values, as shown in the following screenshot:

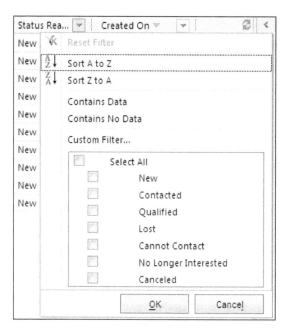

To apply a filter, simply select one of the options from the filter menu and then click **OK**. The filtered data will then be displayed on the grid.

Custom Filter

Creating a custom filter is very straight-forward in Microsoft Dynamics CRM 2011. To demonstrate the use of the custom filter, we are going to create a custom filter to display all contacts whose full name starts with the letter G.

To do this, bring up the filter menu, and then select the **Customer Filter...** option, as shown in the following screenshot:

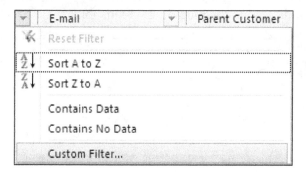

The custom filters dialog box is displayed as shown in the following screenshot. We can specify the conditions for the specific attribute that we want to filter on:

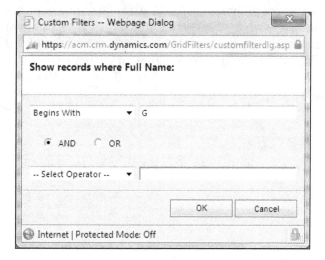

Select **Begin With** from the drop-down list and enter the letter G in the textbox to the right. Lastly, click **OK** to close the dialog box. The filtered data is now displayed on the grid as shown in the following screenshot:

To save a filter, click on the **View** tab on the CRM Ribbon and then click on the **Save Filters** button, as indicated in the following screenshot:

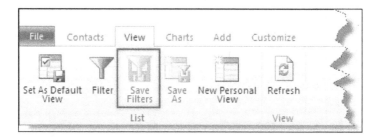

Working with Charts

Charts are new in Microsoft Dynamics CRM 2011. They provides another type of visualization to the end user, and give the end users new analytics and reporting capabilities. Charts are tied to entities; they support out-of-the-box entities and custom entities. CRM comes with charts that all of us can leverage. It also allows us to create custom charts. Charts work with views, filtering, and sub-grids, and we can drill-down on charts.

System Charts

Microsoft CRM 2011 comes with over 50 system charts for the following entities:

- Account
- Activity
- Article
- Campaign
- Case
- Goal

- Lead
- Opportunity
- Order

We can easily view the system for the above entities by following these steps:

1. Navigate to the chart area on the ribbon by clicking on **Charts**.
2. Click on the **Chart Pane** button in the **Layout** group.
3. Click on **Right** in the drop-down menu.

Charts can be displayed on the **Right** or the **Top** of the grid:

Alternatively, we can click on the **Click here to view the chart** pane to the right of the grid as shown in the following screenshot:

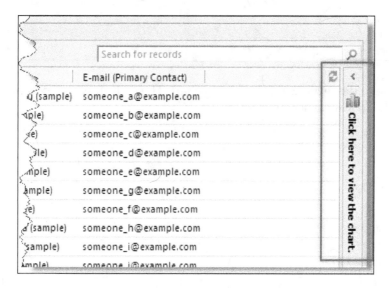

Once we launch the chart pane on the right, we can select the system charts from the chart view list.

Drilldown on Charts

Microsoft Dynamics CRM 2011 allows end users to drill down on charts to further slice and dice data. In addition, the grid also updates the section when we click on the chart. Let's drill down on the **Sales Pipeline** chart that is associated to the **Opportunity** entity.

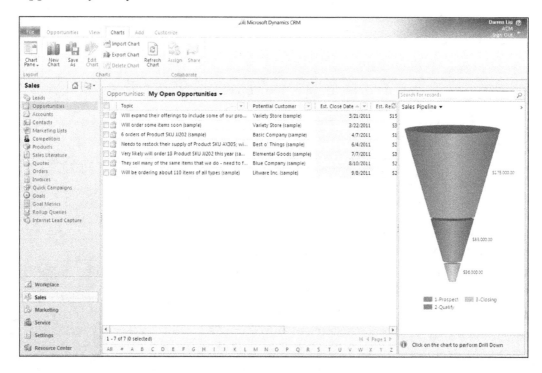

Click on one of the sections on the funnel chart. The drill-down menu appears, as shown in the following screenshot:

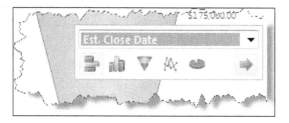

In the **Select Field** list, select **Est. Close Date**, and then click the **Bar** chart option. Click on the **OK** icon to see the result, as shown in the following screenshot:

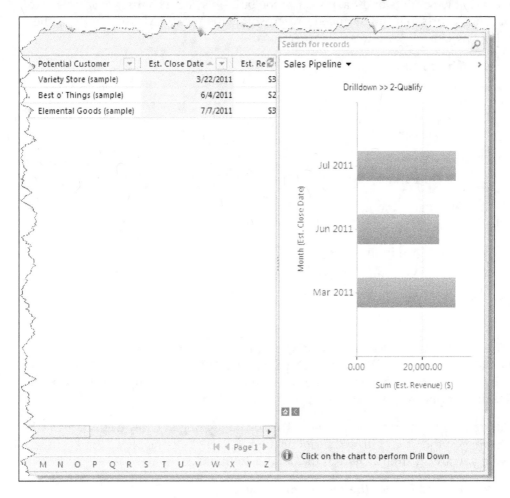

The chart above shows the estimated closed date for all of the opportunities that have revenue between $35,000 and $85,000. As we can see now, the grid updates to show the end user's selection.

Creating Charts

Now that we understand the power of the built-in system charts, we can also create our own charts to fulfill our needs. Microsoft Dynamics CRM 2011 supports the following chart types and set aggregations:

1. Chart Types
    ◦ Pie
    ◦ Column
    ◦ Bar
    ◦ Line
    ◦ Funnel

2. Set Aggregations
    ◦ Average (Avg)
    ◦ Minimum (Min)
    ◦ Maximum (Max)
    ◦ Sum
    ◦ Count

Now let's build a custom chart to display the Compensation by Crew Member. To create a new chart in CRM 2011, navigate to the **ACM Solution**, select **Components | Entities | Crew Member | Charts**, and then click the **New** button. The **Chart Designer** appears.

Alternatively, you can create a new chart by navigating to **Crew Members** in CRM, clicking on the **Chart** tab on the ribbon, and then clicking the **New Chart** button. This way, you are creating a chart in the default solution.

* **Legend Entries (Series): Compensation | Sum**
* **Horizontal (Category) Axis Labels: Crew Member**

The chart name will be automatically generated as: **Compensation by Crew Member**.

Click the **Save and Close** button on the ribbon.

To create a column chart, we don't have to change the chart type. To change the chart type, click on the chart type button under the **Chart Tools** section on the ribbon.

That's it! You just created a chart of the compensation result by crew member.

You can also see individual's compensation by clicking on the relevant part of the chart, and then even drill-down by other columns:

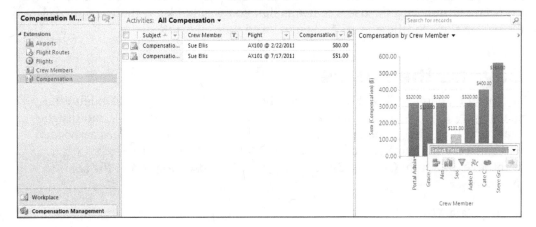

Assign and Share Charts

Once we have created our chart, we can assign it to another end user or share it with another user in the system:

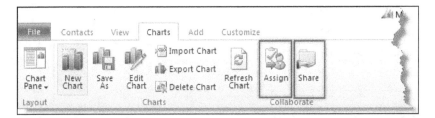

Assign Chart

To assign a chart to another user in the system, click on the **Assign** button. Then select the user or team that you would like to assign it to.

Share Chart

Sharing a chart with another user is similar to sharing records in the system. Click on the **Share** button, add the users or teams that you would like to share it with, select the permissions for these users and teams, and then click **OK**.

Beyond the basics

Microsoft Dynamics CRM 2011 provides the ability for developers to extend the charting capabilities beyond the basics. We can export the chart XML, modify the chart, and then import the chart back to CRM. There are two XML files associated with each chart: Data XML and Presentation XML. Data XML is a Fetch XML used to retrieve data from CRM, and Presentation XML is used to present the chart to the end-user.

1. **Data XML**:

```
<entity name="incident">
  <attribute alias="aggregate_column" name="title"
    aggregate="count" />
  <attribute groupby="true" alias="groupby_column"
    dategrouping="day" name="createdon" />
  <attribute alias="groupby_origin" name="caseorigincode"
    groupby="true" />
</entity>
```

2. **Presentation XML**:

```
<Series ChartType="StackedColumn" Font="{0}, 9.5px"
  LabelForeColor="59, 59, 59"></Series>
</Series>
<ChartAreas>
  <ChartArea BorderColor="White" BorderDashStyle="Solid">
    <AxisY TitleForeColor="59, 59, 59" TitleFont="{0}, 10.5px"
      LineColor="165, 172, 181" IntervalAutoMode="VariableCount">
    </AxisY>
    <AxisX TitleForeColor="59, 59, 59" >
    </AxisX>
```

Because CRM is a .Net application, there are 35 ASP.NET chart types that we can leverage:

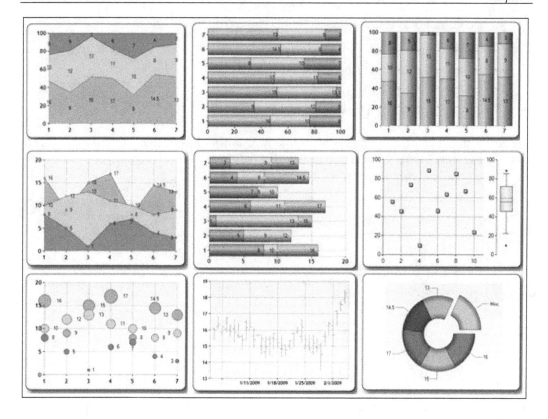

Working with Dashboard

The executives and the management team in a company really like dashboards because a dashboard presents them with critical information related to their business. In the previous version of Microsoft CRM, companies needed to hire developers to build and manage the dashboards because it was not a trivial task. In Microsoft Dynamics CRM 2011, the dashboard capability is built-in to the application. It provides the system dashboards for the end users to use, and also provides the ability for end users to create their own custom dashboard.

System Dashboards

Microsoft Dynamics CRM 2011 provides seven dashboards to cover the customer service, marketing, and sales modules in CRM. System dashboards are controlled by Administrators and they are accessible by all users. Here's the list of these dashboards:

- Customer Service Operations Dashboard
- Customer Service Performance Dashboard

- Customer Service Representative Dashboard

- Marketing Dashboard

- Microsoft Dynamics Overview

- Sales Activity Dashboard

- Sales Performance Dashboard

To access the system dashboards, navigate to **Dashboards** in the **Workplace** area, to display the dashboard view. Then in the view selector, select the desired dashboard to display, as shown in the following screenshot:

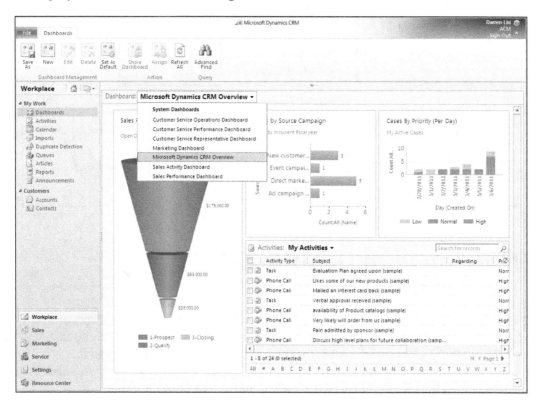

In the dashboard, we have the ability to refresh the chart, view the records associated with the chart, and also have the ability to expand the chart. Just click on the button in the upper right-hand corner of the chart, as indicated in the following screenshot:

Creating Dashboards

Microsoft Dynamics CRM 2011 allows end users to create additional dashboards. These dashboards are known as the User Dashboard, and are all shareable by the users. Before we create a custom dashboard, let's take a look at the components that make up a dashboard in the application. Refer to the following diagram:

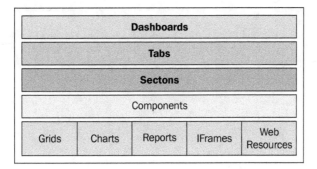

A dashboard contains tabs, sections, and components; components contain grids, charts, reports, iframes,and web resources. Microsoft Dynamics CRM 2011 not only let us include components in the application, but also allows us to include external information, through the use of IFRAMEs. To create a custom dashboard, follow these steps:

1. In the **Workplace** area, click on **Dashboards**. On the ribbon, click the **New** button in the **Dashboard Management** group, as shown in the following screenshot:

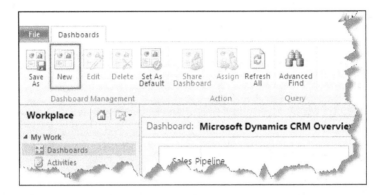

2. Select a Dashboard layout from the **Layout** dialog box, as shown in the following screenshot:

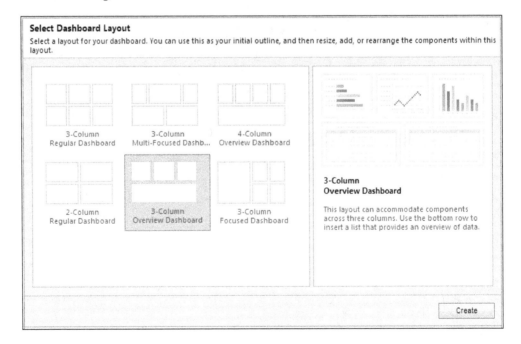

3. Select the desired layout, and then click the **Create** button. In this example, we selected the 3-Column Overview Dashboard. The dashboard layout screen apprears, as shown in the following screenshot:

You can add the following components to the dashboard:

- ° Chart
- ° List
- ° IFrame
- ° Web resource

4. In the **Name** field, enter a name for the dashboard. We are going to name this dashboard **Compensation Overview**.

5. In the top-left section, click the upper-right icon to insert a list, and then select **Compensation | All Compensation**.

6. Delete the upper-middle and upper-right sections, and then click on **Increase Width** to increase the width of the upper-left section.

7. In the bottom section, click the upper-left icon to insert a chart, and then select the **Compensation by Crew Member** chart we just created.

8. Once we finish creating the compoents, simply click **Save** and **Close** to save the dashboard. Now you should be able to see the dashboard in the dashboard list. You can also use it as the default dashboard by clicking the **Set As Default** button on the ribbon.

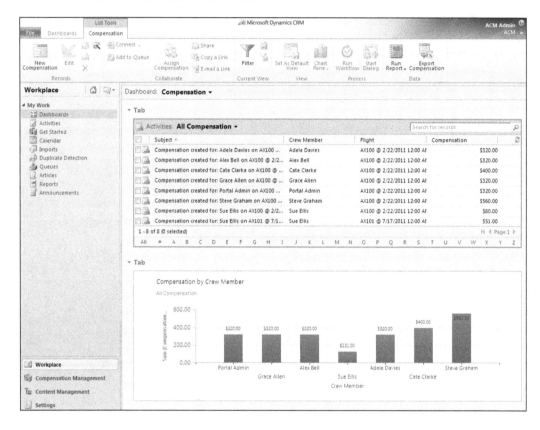

Assign, Share, and Set As Default a Dashboard

Assigning and sharing a dashboard is similar to assigning and sharing charts. Simply click on the **Share Dashboard** button on the ribbon to share the dashboard with different users or teams in the system. Click on the **Assign** button to assign the dashboard to other users and teams. If we keep using the same dashboard and we would like to set it as the default dashboard, click on the **Set As Default** button on the ribbon, as shown in the following screenshot:

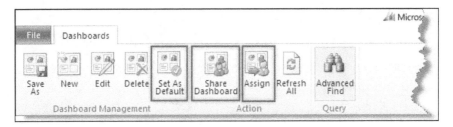

Summary

Microsoft Dynamics CRM 2011 provides new analytics and reporting capabilities to end users. It also provides the ability for the developer to extend the functionality if the out-of-the-box analytics are not able to fulfill the business requirements.

In this chapter, we walked through how to use Filters with the list, how to use Charts, and also how to create Custom Charts. We also covered Dashboards in CRM 2011, and now know how to use the System Dashboards and how to create our own Custom Dashboards. The new business intelligence capabilities in the application allow us to visualize the data better, in order to help us drive more sales, support our customers better, and make better business decisions. In the next chapter, we will introduce how to extend Microsoft Dynamics CRM 2011 in the cloud.

8
Extending Microsoft Dynamics CRM 2011 in the Cloud

Cloud computing is becoming the future of IT. To reduce costs and improve agility and reliability, more and more business applications are moving to the cloud.

In this task, we will introduce Microsoft Cloud offerings and we will set up a portal site on the Windows Azure platform and let it talk to Microsoft CRM 2011 Online. The Azure portal will allow crew members to view and update their information, and see how their compensation is composed. All operations will be synchronized into Microsoft Dynamics CRM 2011 Online. So we are going to cover the following topics:

- Microsoft Cloud Offerings
- CRM 2011 Portal Solutions
- Customer Portal for Microsoft Dynamics CRM 2011
- CRM E-mail Support

Microsoft Cloud offerings

Different vendors have different views about cloud and cloud computing. The Microsoft view is: "An approach to computing that's about Internet scale and connecting to a variety of devices and endpoints. "Microsoft has a comprehensive strategy of cloud computing as Software + Service that spans the application, platform, and infrastructure businesses, both for consumer and enterprise. Currently Microsoft offers three distinct flavors of cloud services:

- **SaaS (Software-as-a-Service)**: Office 365, CRM /ERP Online, Windows Intune

- **PaaS (Platform-as-a-Service)**: Windows Azure platform
- **IaaS (Infrastructure-as-a-Service)**: Hyper-V Private Cloud

For more information about Microsoft Cloud, please visits `http://www.microsoft.com /cloud`.

Windows Azure platform

The Windows Azure platform includes a cloud services operating system and a set of developer services, which provide functionality to build applications that span from consumer Web to enterprise scenarios.

- **Windows Azure** is a cloud services operating system that serves as the development, service hosting, and service management environment for the Windows Azure platform
- **SQL Azure** is a relational data service in the cloud, based on SQL Server
- **Windows Azure AppFabric** provides cloud-based infrastructure services for applications running in the cloud or on premises

Microsoft Office 365

The Microsoft Office 365 platform is a subscription service that combines the familiar Microsoft Office Web Apps with a set of web-enabled tools (such as Exchange 2010 Online, Lync 2010 Online, SharePoint 2010 Online, and so on) that are easy to learn and use, that work with existing hardware, and that are backed up by the robust security, reliability, and control that you need to run a business.

CRM 2011 Portal Solutions

The Microsoft Dynamics CRM 2011 SDK version 5.0.2 and above has the "Portal Developer Guide for Microsoft Dynamics CRM", which makes it easy for developers to build an agile, integrated Microsoft Dynamics CRM Web solution. This sample is in fact coming from the "Customer Portal for Microsoft Dynamics CRM 2011" which is a free version that is provided by Microsoft Dynamics Lab.

Crew Portal

Air-X has their existing IT infrastructure based on Microsoft Windows Servers which is out of date and less maintained. Their stakeholders want to try something new and want their IT staff to focus on Air-X's various business applications, and not on the infrastructure, operating system, or network maintenance. After reviewing and comparing the existing cloud solutions offered on the market, they chose Microsoft Windows Azure platform, which does exactly what they want and, most importantly, is made by Microsoft itself, and therefore surely follows all "Best Practices".

As a starting point, the airline company wants to set up a "Crew Portal" on the Windows Azure platform, to allow crew members to view and update their CRM data from the portal site.

Microsoft Dynamics Marketplace

It's always possible to build a portal solution from scratch, but it's not always efficient to do so. There are many existing CRM solutions that we can use – for free. Microsoft provides an online application store called "Microsoft Dynamics Marketplace" which is the "One Stop Shop" for Dynamics Solutions. The Microsoft Dynamics Marketplace helps you discover innovative applications and professional services provided by Microsoft partners worldwide. You can browse by category or search for solutions. In this book, we use the "Customer Portal for Microsoft Dynamics CRM 2011" as the baseline solution, to demonstrate how the Portal solution works with CRM. Please download the solution from the Microsoft Dynamics Market Place:

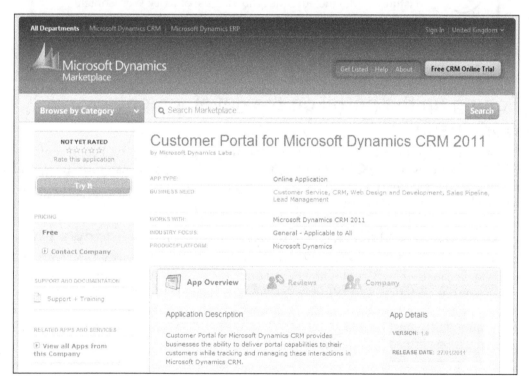

Customer Portal for Microsoft Dynamics CRM 2011

The Customer Portal solution, developed by Microsoft and Adxstudio, provides businesses with the ability to deliver portal capabilities to their customers while tracking and managing these interactions in Microsoft Dynamics CRM. It supports all CRM deployment models: Online, On Premise, and SPLA. The portal site can be created on any Windows Server 2003/2008 + IIS7 or even Windows Azure platform.

The Customer Portal solution comes with Windows Live authentication, but the framework supports any ASP.NET membership provider.

> In this book, we use the free version that is delivered by Adxstudio and Microsoft; Adxstudio also has a commercial version called "Adxstudio Portal" which provides more enterprise features.
>
> Adxstudio Portal includes the following list of tools: Web Content Management, Event Management, Social, Research, Membership, E-Service, and E-Commerce. For additional product information, see `http://www.adxstudio.com/adxstudio-xrm`.

Setting up the portal on the development workspace

Our goal is to deploy the Crew Portal to Windows Azure, and make it communicate with Microsoft Dynamics CRM 2011 Online. So we will test and customize the portal in the local development workspace, then move it to Windows Azure. Either way, we need to do some preparation work first.

Registering the URL on Windows Azure and Windows Live

The Crew Portal website needs a URL in order for crew members to access the website. Because we will deploy the portal on the Windows Azure platform, we need to register the URL prefix on Windows Azure (all Hosted Service URLs end with "cloudapp.net"); and because we use Windows Live ID to authenticate users, the web application URL must be registered on Windows Live, and the domain (Crew Portal URL) must be verified by Windows Live as well.

Microsoft Dynamics CRM 2011 supports integration with the AppFabric Service Bus feature of the Windows Azure platform. For more information about CRM/Azure integration, please visit: `http://msdn.microsoft.com/en-us/library/gg309276.aspx`.

> Windows Azure isn't a free platform; you can see the pricing information here: `http://www.microsoft.com/windowsazure/pricing/`.
>
> However, when developing applications on Windows Azure, you could find some offers at `http://www.microsoft.com/windowsazure/offers/`.

Registering the URL prefix on Windows Azure

1. Go to the Windows Azure portal at `http://windows.azure.com/`.

2. Go to the **Hosted Services, Storage Accounts & CDN** tab, click the **New Hosted Service** button on the ribbon, enter the **Service Name** and **URL** of the Crew Portal, choose your **region**, and then select **Do not deploy**:

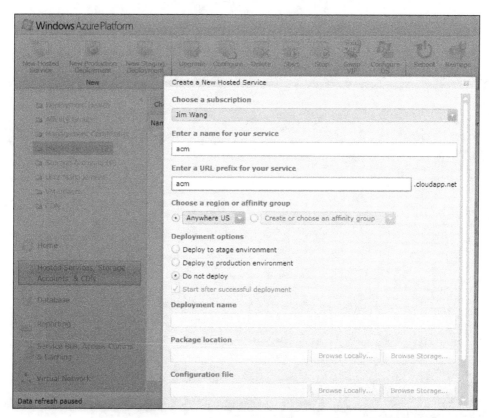

So, in this stage, we registered the URL of the Crew Portal, which is: `http://acm.cloudapp.net`.

 This URL has been registered when writing this book, so you might consider a different URL prefix.

Registering the Web Application on Windows Live

1. Go to `https://live.azure.com/`.

2. Click on the **Add an application** link, specify the **Application name** and **Domain** as **acm.cloudapp.net** and the **Application type** as **Web Application**, and then click the **I accept** button.

 If you see a message of "The domain you specified is already in use by another application", you will have to try another URL prefix on Windows Azure, and use exactly the same URL to register the web application on Windows Live.

3. Click on **Essentials**, and then specify the URLs that are relevant to the portal website. Make sure that the **Return URL** specifies the path **/LiveID.axd**.

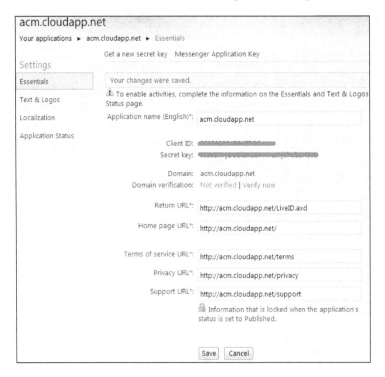

4. Click the **Save** button, and then click on **Verify Now**.

5. Click the **Download** button and then keep the verification file for later use.

Verifying the Domain

1. Create a new Windows Azure Project: ACM Azure in Visual Studio 2010.

2. Select the **ASP.NET Web Role** in the solution.

3. Right-click on the **WebRole1 project**, click **Add | Existing Item**, and then select the verification file.

4. Build the solution and publish ACM Azure to a service package.

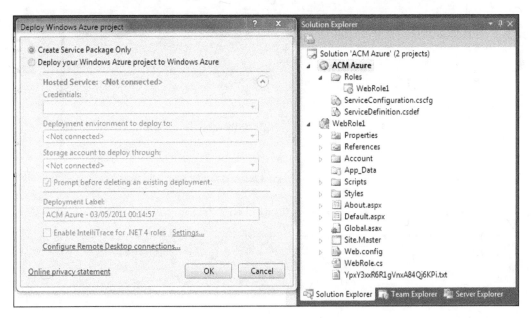

5. Go back to the Hosted Services "ACM" that we just created on Windows Azure, click the **New Production Deployment** button on the ribbon, navigate to the service package files that were created in Step 4, and then click **OK**.

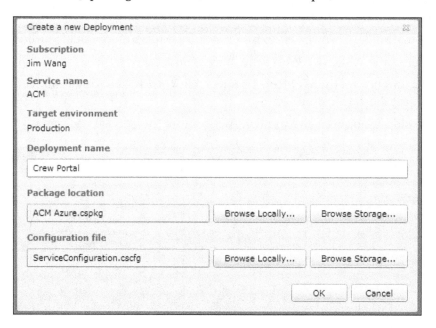

6. After a while, the solution is uploaded to Windows Azure:

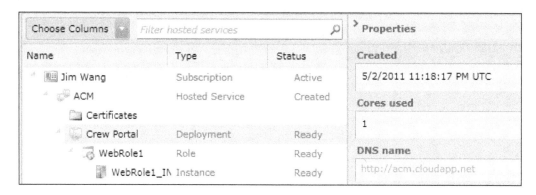

7. Go back to Windows Live to verify the domain.

8. Complete the **Text** and **Logo** settings, and then publish the application.

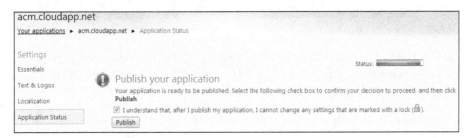

Setting up the DNS zone

We may set up the DNS zone (`cloudapp.net`) on the development workspace to make Windows Live authentication work on the development workspace as well.

Go to the development workspace and run DNS Manager (`dnsmgmt.msc`):

1. Right-click on **Forward Lookup Zones**, in order to set up a New Zone:
   - Primary Zone; Store the zone in Active Directory
   - To all DNS servers running on domain controllers in this domain
   - Zone name: cloudapp.net
   - Allow only secure dynamic updates

2. Right-click on the Zone **cloudapp.net**, and then create a **New Host** to point to this development workspace.

3. Run the the following command:
   ```
   ipconfig /flushdns
   ```

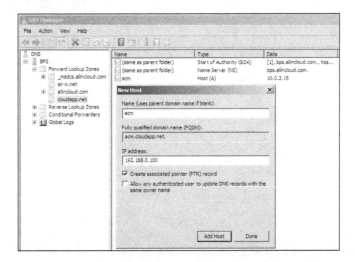

Creating the Crew Portal website

We need to create an IIS website on the development workspace in order to deploy the Customer Portal solution.

Go to IIS Manager (`InetMgr.exe`), and delete the Default website (port 80) if it's not used by any application. Right-click on **Sites**, select **Add Web Site**, and call the new site **Crew Portal**:

- Create a new application pool called **Crew Portal**, make sure the .NET Framework Version is 4.0

- The host name is **acm.cloudapp.net**

 You can choose a different port number if port number 80 is in use.

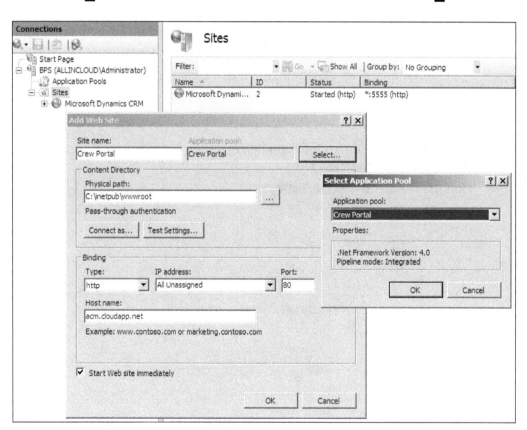

Importing the Portal Solution into Microsoft Dynamics CRM

 You may follow the document *Customer Portal Deployment Guide* in order to complete this task. The document can be found in the Documentation folder.

1. Import and publish the portal solution (`MicrosoftXrmCustomerPortal.zip`) into Microsoft Dynamics CRM on the development workspace.

2. Go to **ACM Settings | Processes**, update the portal sign-up invitation e-mail messages, and change the URL to `http://acm.cloudapp.net/`.

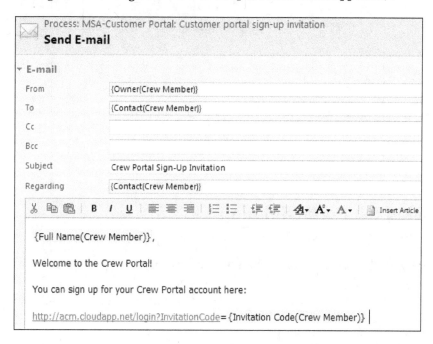

The only two processes that will be used in the ACM system are:

- Customer portal sign-up invitation: This on-demand process will send an invitation e-mail to the crew member.

- Setup basic portal privileges process: This automatic process will add the "Contact Access Permission" of the crew member, to allow the editing of profiles.

3. Use `WebsiteCopy.exe` to upload the initial website content into Microsoft Dynamics CRM.

After performing the last step, the Crew Portal website content should be created in CRM. You can browse it by selecting **ACM Content Management | Websites**, as shown in the following screenshot:

Deploying the Portal Solution

Open the solution file CustomerPortal.sln.

1. Update the connectionString in web.config:

```
<connectionStrings>
<add name="Xrm" connectionString="Url=http://crm-server-name:port/
crm-organization-name; Domain=user-domain; UserName=user-name;
Password=user-password"/>
<add name="Live" connectionString="Application
Id=0000000000000000; Secret=aaaaaaa"/>
</connectionStrings>
```

 Note: You need to replace the Windows Live's Application ID and Secret with your own.

2. Update the portal to **Crew Portal** in `web.config`:

```
<microsoft.xrm.portal>
  <portals>
    <add name="Crew Portal"/>
  </portals>
</microsoft.xrm.portal>
```

3. Rebuild the solution and publish the **CustomerPortal** project to the IIS website that we just created.

4. The Customer Portal has been published on the development workspace server, so that you can access it via the URL: `http://acm.cloudapp.net`.

Testing the Portal

Now that everything is ready, let's go ahead and test the portal site:

1. Go to **ACM | Crew Members**, and create the portal administrator account:
   - **First Name: Portal**
   - **Last Name: Admin**
   - **E-mail**: `portal.admin@air-x.net` (the e-mail is optional in the development workspace)

2. Click the **Create Invitation Code** button on the **Web Authentication** tab of the ribbon, to generate an Invitation Code. You also need to give the **Password Question** and **Password Answer** in order for the validation to work.

3. Click the **Members** link in the navigation pane, add the existing web role to **Portal Admin: Customer Portal Administrators**, and then save the record.

At this stage, the system will trigger the workflow "MSA-Customer Portal: Setup basic portal privileges" to assign the "Contact Access" privilege to Portal Admin.

You also need to manually run the workflow on Portal Admin: "MSA-Customer Portal: Customer portal sign-up invitation". This will send an invitation e-mail to Portal Admin.

Because we haven't set up the Email Router or Outlook, the e-mail won't be sent out. The workaround for development purposes is to open an Internet Browser from the developer server, and browse the following URL to complete the registration process (replace the InvitationCode with Portal Admin's one):

```
http://acm.cloudapp.net/login?InvitationCode=
882FDC25E527472D8B2BC0EC1A45C212
```

You can sign into the portal using any Windows Live ID during this registration verification process. Then, this Live ID will be your portal logon ID. See the next screenshot:

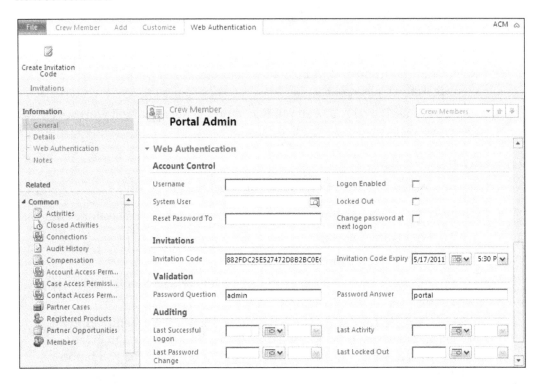

Portal customization

The default portal website is now ready. The next task is to re-brand the website, as well as add custom functions to allow crew members to:

- Update their personal information, which is in the portal already
- Browse the compensation records, to understand how their compensation is composed

Rebranding the portal website

The portal site is very well designed, and you can perform many customizations for the portal site by clicking the blue **Edit** button when logging in with Portal Administrator privileges.

It's fairly easy to rebrand the website through the portal with the Portal Administrator privilege. You can also fundamentally change the look and feel by editing the `Masterpage/CSS/PageLayouts` in Visual Studio.

Following is an example of how to replace the logo with a custom picture:

1. You can create a new page or add a new file to the portal site. Just click the floating editor, and then click the **New** button. Specify the information shown in the following screenshot:

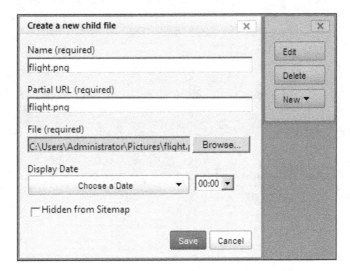

2. The file will then be uploaded into the CRM system. You can find it by navigating to **ACM Content Management | Web Files**. If you create a new page, the page will be stored in the CRM system too, in the Web Pages entity.

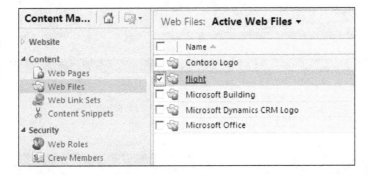

3. You may then use the picture when editing the page:

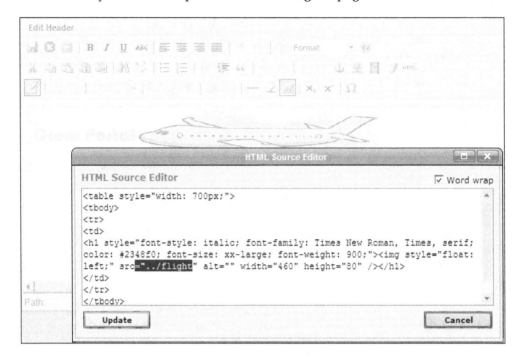

So the portal will look like:

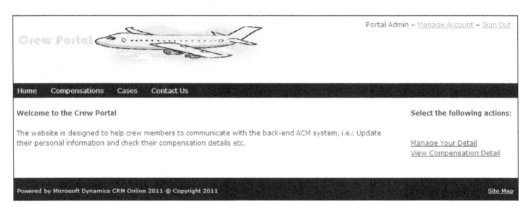

Editing the Profile page

Although this solution provides a flexible non-coding customization experience, for some customizations you do need to look into the code behind in Visual Studio, and make changes accordingly.

In our case, we want to add the MiddleName column to the profile page. So open the solution in Visual Studio 2010, navigate to the **CustomerPortal** | **Pages** | **eService** folder in Solution Explorer, and open the file `Profile.aspx`.

Add the MiddleName section between FirstName and LastName:

```
<div class="row">
<crm:Snippetrunat="server" SnippetName="Profile/MiddleName"
  DefaultText="Middle Name:" />
<asp:TextBox ID="MiddleName" runat="server" />
</div>
```

Then open the file `Profile.aspx.cs`, and add the MiddleName statements in the following classes:

```
protectedvoidPopulateContactForm(Contact contact)
{
  ...
  FirstName.Text = contact.FirstName;
  MiddleName.Text = contact.MiddleName;
  LastName.Text = contact.LastName;
  ...

  if (!ContactPermission.Adx_Write.GetValueOrDefault())
  {
    FirstName.Enabled = false;
    MiddleName.Enabled = false;
    LastName.Enabled = false;

    ...
  }
  ...
}


publicContactSetContactDetails(Contact contact)
{
  ...
  contact.FirstName = FirstName.Text;
  contact.MiddleName = MiddleName.Text;
  contact.LastName = LastName.Text;
  ...
}
```

Next, rebuild the solution and publish it to the development workspace IIS path: `http://acm.cloudapp.net`. You will see that MiddleName now appears on the Profile page.

Next, we also want to change the text of the label "Zip/Postal Code:" to "Postal Code:" You can do this through Visual Studio – that's for sure. However, for such label changes, you can also do it through CRM. Go to **ACM Content Management | Content Snippets**, open the record **Profile/ContactZip**, change its value to **Postal Code**, and save it. This will rewrite the default value in Visual Studio, so you may see that the text has also changed on the Profile page.

Adding a Compensation page

The crew members can see and update their information online, and the information will be updated in to the ACM system via the portal. Now we want to create a page for the crew members to see their compensation per flight.

To create a compensation page, open the Customer Portal solution in Visual Studio 2010, right-click on **CustomerPortal** and select **Pages**, select **Add** | **New Item**, then select **Web Form** using Master Page, change the name to **Compensation.aspx**, and then click **Add**.

In `Compensation.aspx`, change the code to:

```
<%@ Page Language="C#" MasterPageFile="~/MasterPages/Default.
master" AutoEventWireup="true" CodeBehind="Compensation.aspx.cs"
Inherits="Site.Pages.Compensation" %>
<asp:ContentContentPlaceHolderID="Breadcrumbs" runat="server" />
<asp:ContentContentPlaceHolderID="Content" runat="server">
  <asp:GridView ID="CompensationGridView" AutoGenerateColumns="false"
    runat="server">
    <Columns>
      <asp:TemplateFieldHeaderText="Subject">
        <ItemTemplate>
          <asp:Label ID="Label1" Text='<%# Eval("subject")%>'
            runat="server" />
        </ItemTemplate>
      </asp:TemplateField>
      <asp:TemplateFieldHeaderText="Crew Name">
        <ItemTemplate>
          <asp:Label ID="Label2" Text='<%# Eval(
            "acm_CrewMember.Name") %>' runat="server" />
        </ItemTemplate>
      </asp:TemplateField>
      <asp:TemplateFieldHeaderText="Flight Name">
        <ItemTemplate>
          <asp:Label ID="Label3" Text='<%# Eval(
            "acm_Flight.Name") %>' runat="server" />
        </ItemTemplate>
      </asp:TemplateField>
      <asp:TemplateFieldHeaderText="Compensation">
        <ItemTemplate>
          <asp:Label ID="Label4" Text='<%# Eval(
            "acm_Compensation") %>' runat="server" />
        </ItemTemplate>
      </asp:TemplateField>
    </Columns>
  </asp:GridView>
</asp:Content>
<asp:ContentContentPlaceHolderID="ContentBottom" runat="server" />
```

In the file `Compensation.aspx.cs`, change the code to:

```
using System;
usingSystem.Collections.Generic;
usingSystem.Linq;
usingSystem.Web;
usingSystem.Web.UI;
```

```
usingSystem.Web.UI.WebControls;
usingXrm;

namespaceSite.Pages
{
  public partial class Compensation : System.Web.UI.Page
  {
    protected void Page_Load(object sender, EventArgs e)
    {
      //Get the current logon user
      varcurrentUser =
        Microsoft.Xrm.Portal.PortalContext.Current.User;

      if (currentUser != null)
      {
        varxrm = new XrmServiceContext("Xrm");
        //Get user's compensation information
        varmyCompensations = xrm.acm_compensationSet.Where(
          c =>c.acm_CrewMember.Id.Equals(currentUser.Id));
        if (myCompensations != null)
        {
          CompensationGridView.DataSource = myCompensations;
          CompensationGridView.DataBind();
        }
      }
    }
  }
}
```

The Compensation.aspx page also make sure the current signed-in crew member can only see his/her compensation records.

Rebuild the solution, and publish it to the development workspace IIS path: http://acm.cloudapp.net.

The ASPX page is created and published; now we need to create a compensation page on the portal. Sign into the portal using the Portal Admin account. On the floating toolbar, click **New | Child** page, and create a compensation page, as shown in the following screenshot:

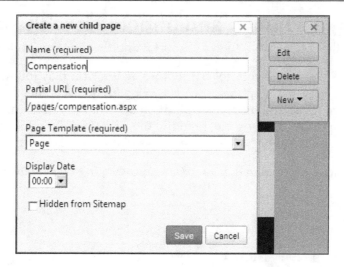

On the primary navigation toolbar, click **Add**, and then create a **Compensation** link:

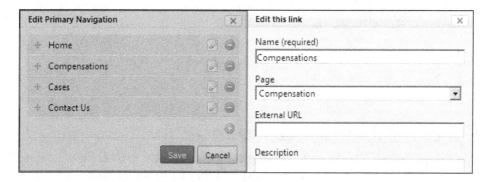

Now that the compensation link has been added, you can click and see compensation information related to the currently-signed-in user. This is just a demo of the page; you can add whatever you want to see, from CRM onto the Crew Portal.

Exporting a solution and bringing it to the cloud

Now we have the solution, we need to export it and then import it into CRM Online.

To deploy the Crew Portal website to Windows Azure, you may follow the document *Customer Portal Deployment Guide_Azure* (in the Documentation folder). Because we have registered the web application on Windows Live and Azure, you don't need to repeat those steps—just modify the Visual Studio solution, and add the Windows Azure role and deploy it to the Azure platform.

The major change is to update the `connectionString` in the file `web.config`:

```
<connectionStrings>
  <add name="Xrm"
    connectionString="Url=https://crmurl.crm.dynamics.com;
    UserName=wlid@hotmail.com; Password=wlidpassword;
    Device ID=your-device-id;
    Device Password=your-device-password"/>
  <add name="Live" connectionString="Application
    Id=0000000000000000; Secret=aaaaaaa"/>
</connectionStrings>
```

 Note: You need to replace the Windows Live Application ID and Secret with your own.

CRM E-mail support

Microsoft Dynamics CRM 2011 Online doesn't come with the E-mail Router capability. By default it uses Microsoft Dynamics CRM for Outlook to send and receive CRM e-mails, which does work if you have the CRM for Outlook software installed and configured, and can keep Outlook open for sending and receiving CRM e-mails.

In our case, Air-X has chosen Microsoft Office 365 as their Business-IT platform. This includes a set of business productivity tools, including is Office Web Apps, Exchange Online, Lync Online, and SharePoint Online. So we can use Exchange Online plus CRM E-mail Router to support CRM e-mail messages.

CRM E-mail Router

Microsoft Dynamics CRM E-mail Router is a software component that creates an interface between Microsoft Dynamics CRM and Microsoft Exchange Server (2003, 2007, 2010, and Online) and an SMTP or POP3-compliant E-mail server. After the E-mail Router has been installed, it transfers e-mail messages to Microsoft Dynamics CRM, and sends outgoing e-mail messages that users created in Microsoft Dynamics CRM.

Our plan is to install the CRM E-mail Router software on a local server that has Internet access (we are not going to introduce how to set up a real server here, but will just do it on our development workspace), and configure it to communicate with CRM Online and Exchange Online.

The CRM E-mail Access is configured per user. Go to **ACM Settings | Administration | Users**; you will see the E-mail Access Configuration window. This has the Outlook option for both incoming and outgoing e-mail messages, by default. Change both to use E-mail Router.

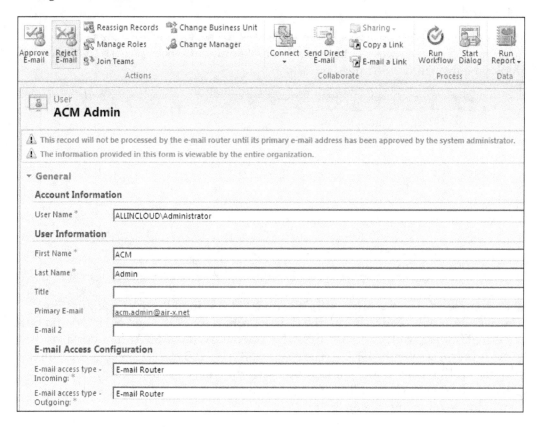

Note: The Primary E-mail address is the user's e-mail address in **Office 365 | Exchange Online**. This must be approved by the system administrator.

Setting up CRM E-mail Router with Office 365 Exchange Online

The Microsoft Dynamics CRM 2011 E-mail Router can be downloaded from
`http://www.microsoft.com/downloads/en/details.aspx?FamilyID=a995f6ad-0099-42fd-9b22-cf7b3d40a2bf`.

The E-mail router supports both 32 bit and 64 bit Windows Server 2008 or Windows 7. Because our development workspace is using 64 bit Window Server 2008 R2, that's good.

During the installation process, choose to install the service only, because we don't have the Exchange server deployed in this development workspace, so the Rule Deployment Wizard won't need it.

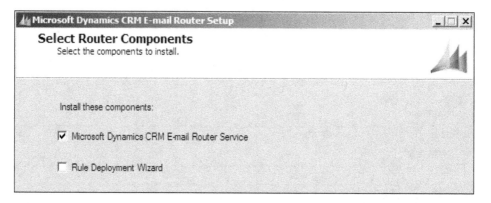

Once completed, run the Microsoft Dynamics CRM E-mail Router Configuration Manager. You will need to set up the E-mail profiles for POP and SMTP. To find out the E-mail settings of Exchange Online, log on to the Office 365 Admin Portal as the CRM Admin user via the URL `https://portal.microsoftonline.com`, and then click the **Options** link under the **Outlook** section. Then click the **Settings for POP, IMAP, and SMTP access...** link. You can then see the POP and SMTP settings, as shown in the following screenshot:

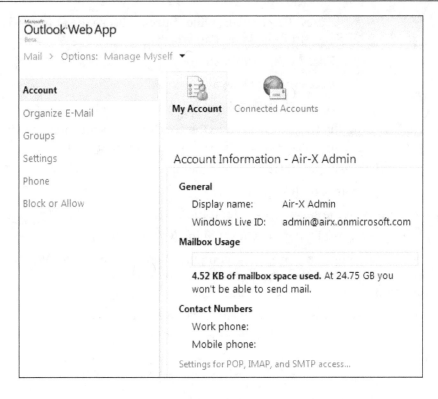

1. On the **Configuration Profile** tab, create two profiles: one for POP and one for SMTP, using the following settings:
   - Profile Name: POP
     - Direction: Incoming
     - E-mail Server Type: Exchange Online
     - Protocol: Exchange Web Services
     - Location: Use Autodiscover
     - Access Credentials: Other Specified (use the Office 365 admin Sign-In E-mail and Password)
     - Network Port: 995 (on the Advanced tab)
   - Profile Name: SMTP
     - Direction: Outgoing
     - E-mail Server Type: Exchange Online
     - Protocol: Exchange Web Services
     - Location: Use Autodiscover

    °   Access Credentials: Other Specified (use the Office 365 admin Sign-In E-mail and Password)

    °   User Type: Administrator

    °   Access Type: Delegate Access

    °   Network Port: 587 (on the Advanced tab)

2. After creating the two profiles, go to the **Deployments** tab, and specify the type, location, and access credentials of the CRM deployment.

3. There are three types of CRM deployment:

   - My company (On-premise)
   - An online service provider (SPLA)
   - Microsoft Dynamics CRM Online (CRM Online)

4. For development/test proposes, you may choose the first one: **My company**, and then point it to the local development workspace, at: `http://CrmDiscov eryServer:<port>/<OrganizationName>`.

5. Next, set the **Access Credentials** to **Local System Account**, and choose POP and SMTP for the incoming and outgoing profiles.

On the production server, when you point it to CRM Online, the URL format would be `https://dev.crm.dynamics. com/<OrganizationUniqueName>`.

Note that OrganizationUniqueName isn't the OrganizationName, you can get the unique name by going to **CRM Online | Settings | Customizations | Developer Resources**. Then specify the CRM Online Sign-In User Name and Password of a system user. Use the same POP and SMTP profiles.

The E-mail Router should only be configured against Online, On-Premise, or SPLA. It is not designed to support both CRM On-Premise and CRM Online deployments concurrently.

---

6. Now go to the last tab of the E-mail Router Configuration Manager: **Users, Queues, and Forward Mailboxes**. Select the CRM deployment that you set up in the previous step, and then click the **Load Data** button. In the **Users and Queues** window, you will see a list of all CRM users who have selected the E-mail Router option in the E-mail Access Configuration.

7. Select those user accounts, and then click the **Test Access** button. If you see both SMTP and POP are a success, click the **Publish** button to save the E-mail Router configuration settings, and then close the application. See the following screenshots.

Note: The Primary Email address must be approved by the CRM system administrator before it can be seen by the E-mail Router application.

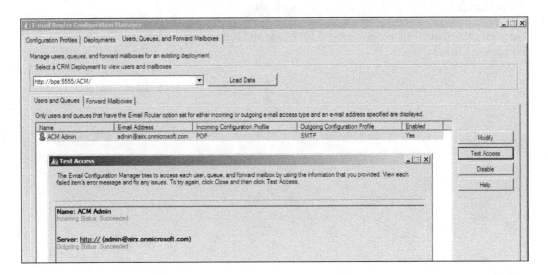

8. In production, the user should get an invitation e-mail directly from CRM Online to their Exchange Online mailbox:

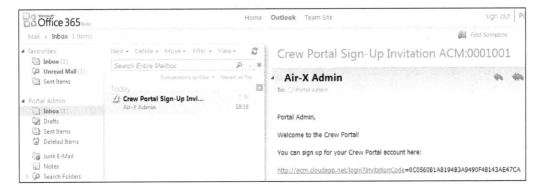

Summary

In this chapter, we briefly introduced the Microsoft Cloud Offering. We demonstrated how to use the Customer Portal solution to build and customize a Crew Portal for Microsoft Dynamics CRM 2011.

We also introduced how to set up CRM E-mail Router support with Office 365 | Exchange Online.

9

Sitemap and Ribbon Customization

In most projects, we need to change the application navigation to add or remove modules that are related to the project. In addition, we are often asked to modify the ribbon to add or remove buttons, groups, and tabs. Microsoft Dynamics CRM 2011 introduces the ribbon as the primary location of controls that are used to perform actions within the application. In this chapter, we are going to cover the following topics:

- Working with the SiteMap
- CRM 2011 Ribbon Overview
- Working with the Ribbon

Working with SiteMap

The CRM application navigation pane is controlled in the SiteMap, which is a node in the `customizations.xml` file of an unmanaged solution. The SiteMap is also affected by the current user's security privileges. That is, if the current user doesn't have the read access to an entity specified in the SiteMap, then that navigation option will not be displayed to the user. In addition to that, SiteMap has its own privilege settings, which is very useful for specifying privilege requirements to view a page that is not related to a specific entity.

```Xml
<Privilege
 Entity=String
 Privilege=[Read|Write|Append|AppendTo|Create|Delete|Share|Assign|All|AllowQuickCampaign|UseInternetMarketing]
/>
```

SiteMap XML references

The following XML elements are used to customize the SiteMap. For detailed information please reference the CRM 2011 SDK:

Element	Description
`<Area>`	Specifies an area that appears in the navigation pane.
`<Description>`, `<Descriptions>`	Contains a (set of) localizable descriptions for the parent element.
`<Group>`	Specifies a group of subareas.
`<Privilege>`	Controls whether a subarea is displayed, based on privileges available in any security roles assigned to the user.
`<SiteMap>`	Specifies the root node for the site map.
`<SubArea>`	Specifies a navigation option within an area, and defines what will be displayed in the main pane of the application when selected.
`<Title>`, `<Titles>`	Specifies a (set of) localizable titles for the parent element.

The following diagram shows the out-of-the-box navigation pane:

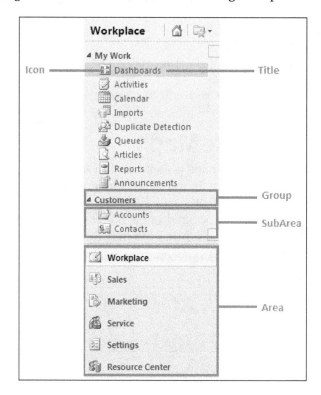

SiteMap configuration options

The SiteMap customization can be applied on both the CRM web client and the Outlook client. The following sections explain the configurations that are available in SiteMap.

Changing Labels

The CRM out-of-the-box SiteMap uses the `ResourceId` attribute for system entities. If you want to rename a label, use the "Title" attribute to specify the text which will override the ResourceId attribute value. But do not change the ResourceId value directly.

Changing Icons

You can use the "Icon" attribute to specify a new icon in both the `<Area>` and `<SubArea>` elements. In CRM 2011, you can also specify the icon by using the Web resource.

Note: When referencing the GIF/JPG/PNG Web resource, use the Web resource directive (`$webresource:`), that is `Icon="$webresource:acm_/icons/MyIcon.png"`, where the name of the Web resource is `acm_/icons/MyIcon.png`. The directive will create a dependency so that the Web resource cannot be deleted as long as your SiteMap element requires it.

Adding or removing elements

You can edit the XML to add or remove elements as required in the SiteMap; however it's the best practice to use security role privileges to control access to areas of the application.

Adding New Pages/Links

You can specify a target URL for Area/SubArea or Group by using the "URL" attribute, which can reference a page on an external Web site or an HTML Web resource. You can also use the `PassParams` attribute to pass information (organization name, user language code, and organization language code) to the target URL as parameters. So the final URL could look like: `http://myserver/mypage.aspx?orgna me=AirlineCompensationManagement&userlcid=1033&orglcid=1033`.

Note: When referencing the HTML Web resource, use the Web resource directive (`$webresource:`), that is `Icon="$webresource:acm_/Pages/MyPage.htm"`, where the name of the HTML Web resource is `acm_/Pages/MyPage.htm`. The directive will create a dependency so that the Web resource cannot be deleted as long as your SiteMap element requires it.

Grouping Links within Areas

You can group SubAreas by using the `<Group>` element. You must specify the attribute `ShowGroups = "true"` in the parent `<Area>` element in order to show the group name.

Customizing the Get Started Pane

CRM 2011 provides an excellent guide and template to help you get started. You can also use the template (which can be found in the `SDK\Resources\GetStartedPaneTemplate`) to create your own **CRM GetStarted** page for the following user groups:

- `GetStartedPanePath`
- `GetStartedPanePathAdmin`
- `GetStartedPanePathOutlook`
- `GetStartedPanePathAdminOutlook`

Note: If only the `GetStartedPanePath` attribute value is specified, that page will be shown for all users and client types.

Changing the Workplace profile options

Groups within the Workplace area can use the `IsProfile` attribute to make these groups available as options in the users' personal options. When the `IsProfile` attribute is set to true, people will be able to choose which of the groups in that area they want to be displayed. They can choose not to display groups that are not relevant to their work by going to **ACM Files | Options | Workplace**:

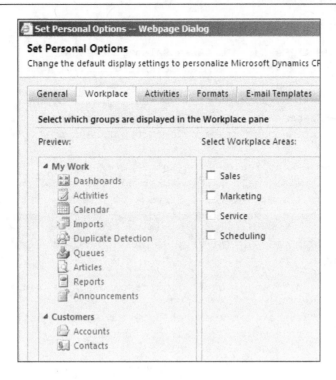

ACM SiteMap customization

Now that we have all of the entities, we need to change the CRM application navigation pane by using the SiteMap.

In the ACM system, we want to keep the Workplace and Settings area, and also add a new area called **Compensation Management**.

Go to **ACM Settings | Solutions | ACMSolution | Components**, and then click **Add Existing | SiteMap**. The default SiteMap is added to the ACM solution.

To edit the SiteMap, we will need to export the solution. Click **Export Solution** on the toolbar, and then export the Customization as an unmanaged solution.

Unzip the solution file, open the `customizations.xml` file, and locate the SiteMap node at `ImportExportXml/SiteMap/SiteMap`, (or search for `<SiteMap>`).

 Keep the solution ZIP file as a backup.

Remove the following code fragments:

```
<Group Id="SFA" ResourceId="Area_Sales"...... </Group>
<Group Id="MA" ResourceId="Area_Marketing"...... </Group>
<Group Id="CS" ResourceId="Area_Service"...... </Group>
<Group Id="SM" ResourceId="Area_Scheduling"...... </Group>
<Group Id="Customers" ResourceId="Group_Customers"...... </Group>
<Group Id="Extensions" ResourceId="Group_Extensions"...... </Group>


<Area Id="SFA" ResourceId="Area_Sales"...... </Area>
<Area Id="MA" ResourceId="Area_Marketing"...... </Area>
<Area Id="CS" ResourceId="Area_Service"...... </Area>
<Area Id="ResourceCenter" ResourceId="Area_ResourceCenter"...... </Area>
```

Add a new Area to include Airport, Flight Route, Flight, Crew Member (contact), and Compensation:

```
<Area Id="acm_sitemap" Icon="/_imgs/resourcecenter_24x24.gif"
  Title="Compensation Management">
  <Group Id="Extensions" ResourceId="Group_Extensions">
    <SubArea Id="acm_airport" Entity="acm_airport"
      Icon="/_imgs/ico_18_4009.gif" />
    <SubArea Id="acm_flightroute" Entity="acm_flightroute"
      Icon="/_imgs/ico_18_history.gif" />
    <SubArea Id="acm_flight" Entity="acm_flight"
      Icon="/_imgs/ico_18_9600.png" />
    <SubArea Id="nav_conts" Entity="contact" />
    <SubArea Id="nav_activities" Entity="activitypointer"
      Title="Compensation" Icon="/_imgs/ico_18_1022.gif"
      Url="/_root/homepage.aspx?etc=10035" />
  </Group>
</Area>
```

> Notice that the compensation link is an activity pointer, which has a URL property that contains the `objecttypecode` of the compensation entity.
>
> You can also find the entity's `objecttypecode` in the SiteMap by searching the keyword: `acm_compensation`. It could be different in your system.

```
<Entity>
  <Name LocalizedName="Compensation" OriginalName="Compensation">acm_compensation</Name>
  <ObjectTypeCode>10035</ObjectTypeCode>
  <EntityInfo>
    <entity Name="acm_compensation">
```

Next, compress the `customizations.xml` file with the `[Content_Types].xml` and `solution.xml` into a ZIP file and go to **ACM Settings | Solutions | Import**, to import the new solution package and publish it.

You will see the application navigation pane has been updated:

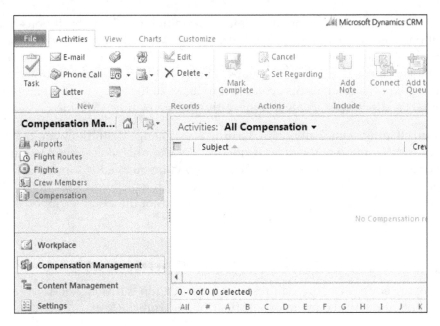

CRM 2011 Ribbon overview

The navigation within Microsoft Dynamics CRM 2011 has completely changed. Similar to the Microsoft Office application, Microsoft Dynamics CRM 2011 introduces the ribbon, as shown below, as the primary location of controls that are used to perform actions in the application:

There are some key concepts that you need to understand, and also common tasks you will need to perform, when customizing the ribbon. In order to customize the ribbon, it would help if you have a background in XML because as of now when we at the time of writing this book, there are no tools available for customizing the ribbon.

Microsoft Dynamics CRM contains a default definition for all of the ribbons in the application. You can export and view the current XML code that defines the ribbon for your own CRM organization, but you can't update the XML directly. Keep in mind that if you want to change the ribbon, you need to define how you want it changed. All of the changes that you want to make to the ribbon will be stored in RibbonDiffXml, which is located in the entity customization XML file.

When you customize your ribbon by writing your change definition, you need to reference the definition of the default ribbons. For example, if you need to add a button or a group next to an existing ribbon element, you need to know the ID values for those elements, as well as the sequence order with which you will control the relative position of the elements. To get the ID values of the existing ribbon elements, you need to export the ribbon definition.

Exporting Default Ribbon definitions

Exporting the entities ribbon requires a tool provided in the Microsoft CRM SDK. Please follow the steps below to export the ribbons from CRM.

> Note: In order to run the ribbon export tool, you need to have Visual Studio 2010 installed on your local computer. Also you need to download and extract the latest Microsoft CRM 2011 SDK to your local computer. To download the CRM 2011 SDK, please visit the Microsoft Download Site at http://www.microsoft.com/download/en/details.aspx?id=24004. The ribbon export tool is in the \SampleCode\CS\Client\Ribbon\ExportRibbonXml\ ExportedRibbonXml folder.

1. Double-click the exportribbonxml.sln file to launch the Visual Studio project.

2. Press *F5* to run the console application.

3. Select 0 to add New Server Configuration and then enter the CRM server information.

4. Enter your User Name and Password.

5. Select the Organization that you would like to export the ribbon definitions to.

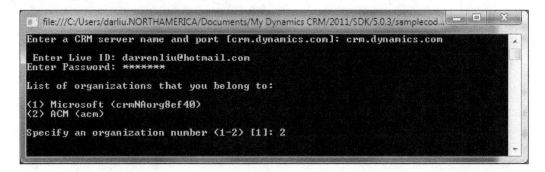

6. Press Enter to exit the application.

When the application has finished exporting the ribbon definitions, all of the ribbon definitions for the entities will be available in the exportedribbonxml folder where your project is placed. Let's take a look at the different types of ribbons before we start customizing the ribbon for our ACM system. We'll need to refer back to the ribbon definitions that we exported here when we customize the ribbon in the samples below.

Entity Ribbons

All entities in Microsoft Dynamics CRM 2011 leverage the same Entity Ribbon Template as the base ribbon definition. Each system entity has a separate RibbonDiffXml definition that builds upon the entity ribbon template definition. The base ribbon definition is stored in a file called applicationribbon.xml.

Note: The `applicationribbon.xml` file is one of the files exported using the `ExportRibbonXml` application mentioned above.

```xml
applicationribbon.xml ×
<RibbonDefinitions>
  <RibbonDefinition>
    <UI>
      <Jewel Id="Mscrm.Jewel" Command="Mscrm.Jewel" Alt="$Resources:Ribbon.Jewel.Tooltip" LabelText="$Resources:Rib
        <Menu Id="Mscrm.Jewel.Menu">
          <MenuSection Id="Mscrm.Jewel.MenuSectionSave" Sequence="9" DisplayMode="Menu16">
            <Controls Id="Mscrm.Jewel.ControlsSave">
              <FlyoutAnchor Id="Mscrm.Jewel.SaveMenu" Command="Mscrm.Jewel.SaveMenu" LabelText="$Resources:Ribbon.J
                <Menu Id="Mscrm.Jewel.SaveMenu.Menu">
                  <MenuSection Id="Mscrm.Jewel.SaveMenu.MenuSection1" Sequence="10" DisplayMode="Menu16">
                    <Controls Id="Mscrm.Jewel.SaveMenu.Controls">
                      <Button Id="Mscrm.Jewel.SaveMenu.Save" Command="Mscrm.SavePrimary" Sequence="10" LabelText="$
                      <Button Id="Mscrm.Jewel.SaveMenu.SaveAndClose" Command="Mscrm.SaveAndClosePrimary" Sequence="
                      <Button Id="Mscrm.Jewel.SaveMenu.SaveAndNew" Command="Mscrm.SaveAndNewPrimary" Sequence="30">
                    </Controls>
                  </MenuSection>
                </Menu>
              </FlyoutAnchor>
            </Controls>
          </MenuSection>
          <MenuSection Id="Mscrm.Jewel.MenuSection1" Sequence="10" DisplayMode="Menu16">
            <Controls Id="Mscrm.Jewel.Controls1">
              <FlyoutAnchor Id="Mscrm.Jewel.NewMenu.NewActivity" Sequence="10" Command="Mscrm.Enabled" LabelText="$
              <FlyoutAnchor Id="Mscrm.Jewel.NewMenu.NewRecord" Sequence="20" Command="Mscrm.Enabled" Image16by16="/
            </Controls>
          </MenuSection>
          <MenuSection Id="Mscrm.Jewel.Section2" Sequence="20" DisplayMode="Menu16">
            <Controls Id="Mscrm.Jewel.Controls2">
              <Button Id="Mscrm.Jewel.FormProperties" Command="Mscrm.Jewel.FormProperties" LabelText="$Resources:Me
              <Button Id="Mscrm.Jewel.PrintPreview" Command="Mscrm.Jewel.PrintPreview" LabelText="$Resources:Ribbon
            </Controls>
```

Grid Ribbons

The entity grid ribbon is a collection of tabs that have an ID attribute value beginning with `Mscrm.HomepageGrid.<entity logical name>`. For example, the tab with the text "Contacts" on a contact entity grid is `Mscrm.HomepageGrid.contact.MainTab`. All of the tabs displayed on the account entity grid will have an ID value that begins with `Mscrm.HomepageGrid.contact`. Please take a look at the following screenshot:

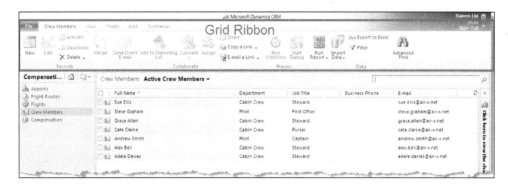

Sub Grid Ribbons

When a list of records for a different entity is displayed within a sub-grid on the form of another entity or in a chart, the ribbon will change when the user places the cursor in the grid. Please take a look at the next screenshot.

The entity sub-grid ribbon is a contextual group with a collection of tabs that have an ID attribute value beginning with `Mscrm.SubGrid.<entity logical name>`. For example, the tab with the text "Contacts" on the contact entity sub-grid is `Mscrm.SubGrid.contact.MainTab`.

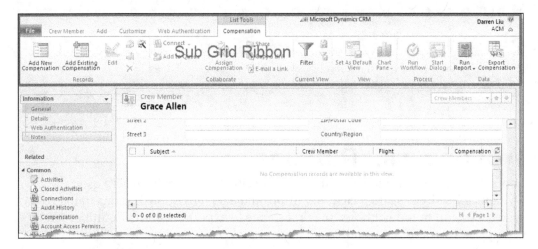

Form Ribbons

Each entity can have multiple forms. You can define changes to the form ribbon for all forms for that entity by adding your definition at the entity level in `//ImportExportXml/Entities/Entity/RibbonDiffXml`. If you would like to change the ribbon for the specific form, you need to modify `RibbonDiffXml` at this location: `//ImportExportXml/Entities/Entity/FormXml/forms/systemform/form/RibbonDiffXml`.

The entity form ribbon is a collection of tabs that have an ID attribute value beginning with `Mscrm.Form.<entity logical name>`. For example, the tab with the label Contact on the contact entity form is `Mscrm.Form.contact.MainTab`. All of the tabs displayed on the contact entity form will have an ID value that begins with `Mscrm.Form.contact`.

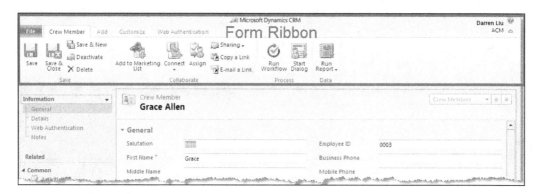

Working with Ribbons

I hope that you now understand the different ribbon types within Microsoft Dynamics CRM. Let's add a custom button, and also hide some buttons in the ACM system. To add or hide buttons, the first step is to export the entity definition. In this example, we are going to modify the Crew Member entity ribbon.

Note that it is recommended to create a solution for each of the entities for which you want to modify the ribbon. That way, the size of the customization file will be smaller and easier to manage. Also, for the purpose of editing the ribbon, you do not have to include the required component in the solution that you are going to export.

Exporting Ribbon definitions

1. Navigate to **Settings** and then click on **Customization**.

2. Click **Solutions**.

3. Click **New**.

   Enter the **Display Name**, **Unique Name**, and **Version number**. In our example, we are going to enter "Contact" for Display Name, select the default ACM publisher, and "1.0.0.0" as the version number:

4. Select **Publisher**.

5. Click the **Save** icon.

6. Click on **Add Existing**, and then click **Entity**.

7. Select the **Crew Member** entity and then click **OK**. Don't include the required components if you see the **Missing Required Components** window.

8. Click on **Add Existing**, and then select **Application Ribbons**.

9. Click on **Save and Close** to save the solution.

10. Select the solution that you want to export, and then click **Export**.

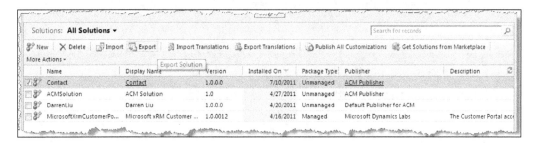

11. If you published the recent changes that you made to that entity, click **Publish All Customizations**. Otherwise, click **Next**.

12. Select the **Unmanaged** option, and then click **Export**.

13. Save the customization to your local desktop.

 Note: The file name for this solution is `RibbonSolution.zip`.

Adding a To Button to the Application Ribbon

In the previous chapter, we have created a dialog to help agents to add flight activities for the ACM system. Now let's walk through the steps for adding a button to the application ribbon so that it shows up on all ACM entity ribbons within the ACM system.

The first step is to upload the images and the JScript for the ribbon button to the Web Resources library. Please follow the steps below.

We are going to upload the following three web resources:

Name	Display Name	Type
/images/LaunchDialog16x16. png	/images/LaunchDialog16x16.png	PNG Format
/images/LaunchDialog32x32. png	/images/LaunchDialog32x32.png	PNG Format
/scripts/globalfunctions.js	/scripts/globalfunctions.js	Script(JScript)

1. Navigate to the **Ribbon Solution**.

2. Click on Web Resources in the left most navigation pane.

3. Click the **New** button on the grid menu.

4. Enter `/images/LaunchDialog16x16.png` in the **Name** textbox.

5. Enter `/images/LaunchDialog16x16.png` in the **Display N**ame textbox.

6. Select **PNG** format in the **Type** drop-down box.

7. Click the **Browse...** button, and then navigate to and select `LaunchDialog16x16.png` from your local computer.

8. Click **Save and Close** to close the new **Web Resource** window.

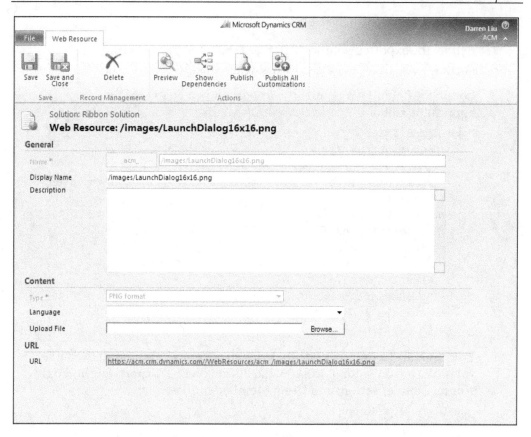

9. Repeat the steps above to upload the second image: `LaunchDialog32x32.png`.

10. Repeat the steps above to upload the `globalfunction.js` file. Select `Script (JScript)` from the **Type** drop-down box.

    Copy and paste the following JScript code into the file `globalfunction.js`:

    ```
    function acm_LaunchDialog() {
      // Replace with your Dialog Id
      var dialogId = "D5C4E511-C013-4455-AC4C-31A80766C925";
        // Replace

      window.open(Xrm.Page.context.getServerUrl() +
        "/cs/dialog/rundialog.aspx?DialogId=" + escape(dialogId) +
        "&EntityName=" + "systemuser" + "&ObjectId=" +
        Xrm.Page.context.getUserId());
    }
    ```

The second step is to modify the ribbon:

1. Extract the exported solution ZIP file, `RibbonSolution.zip`.

2. Open the `customizations.xml` file using any text editor.

3. Locate the default `RibbonDiffXml` node, shown below for the application ribbon:

```
<RibbonDiffXml>
  <CustomActions />
  <Templates>
    <RibbonTemplates Id="Mscrm.Templates"></RibbonTemplates>
  </Templates>
  <CommandDefinitions />
  <RuleDefinitions>
    <TabDisplayRules />
    <DisplayRules />
    <EnableRules />
  </RuleDefinitions>
  <LocLabels />
</RibbonDiffXml>
```

4. Edit the Rule Definition node to define the display rule, and then enable rules. We are only going to show the button on the **Airport**, **Flight**, **Flight Route**, **Compensation**, and **Crew Member** entities.

```
<RuleDefinitions>
  <TabDisplayRules />
  <DisplayRules>
    <DisplayRule Id="acm.all.form.CustomGroup.
      LaunchDialog.Display">
      <OrRule>
        <Or>
          <EntityRule EntityName="acm_airport" />
        </Or>
        <Or>
          <EntityRule EntityName="acm_compensation" />
        </Or>
        <Or>
          <EntityRule EntityName="acm_flight" />
        </Or>
        <Or>
          <EntityRule EntityName="acm_flightroute" />
        </Or>
        <Or>
          <EntityRule EntityName="contact" />
```

```
          </Or>
        </OrRule>
      </DisplayRule>
    </DisplayRules>
    <EnableRules />
  </RuleDefinitions>
```

5. Edit the `LocLabels` node to set the localized labels.

```
<LocLabels>
  <LocLabel Id="acm.all.form.CustomGroup.LaunchDialog">
    <Titles>
      <Title languagecode="1033"
        description="Launch ACM Dialog" />
    </Titles>
  </LocLabel>
  <LocLabel Id="acm.all.form.CustomGroup.LaunchDialog.Text">
    <Titles>
      <Title languagecode="1033"
        description="Launch ACM Dialog" />
    </Titles>
  </LocLabel>
</LocLabels>
```

6. Edit the `CommandDefinition` node to add your commands.

```
<CommandDefinitions>
  <CommandDefinition Id="acm.all.form.CustomGroup.
    LaunchDialog.Controls.Launch.Command">
  <EnableRules />
    <DisplayRules />
    <Actions>
      <JavaScriptFunction
        Library="$webresource:acm_/scripts/globalfunctions.js"
        FunctionName="acm_LaunchDialog">
      </JavaScriptFunction>
    </Actions>
  </CommandDefinition>
  <CommandDefinition
    Id="acm.all.form.CustomGroup.LaunchDialog.Command">
    <EnableRules />
    <DisplayRules>
      <DisplayRule
        Id="acm.all.form.CustomGroup.LaunchDialog.Display" />
    </DisplayRules>
    <Actions />
  </CommandDefinition>
</CommandDefinitions>
```

7. Edit the `CustomActions` element to add your custom actions—one for each of the buttons that you are going to create.

```xml
<CustomActions>
  <CustomAction Id="acm.all.form.CustomGroup.LaunchDialogAction"
    Location="Mscrm.Form.{!EntityLogicalName}.MainTab.
    Groups._children" Sequence="1007">
  <CommandUIDefinition>
    <Group Id="acm.all.form.CustomGroup.LaunchDialog"
      Command="acm.all.form.CustomGroup.LaunchDialog.Command"
      Title="$LocLabels:acm.all.form.CustomGroup.LaunchDialog"
      Sequence="1008" Template="Mscrm.Templates.Flexible2">
      <Controls Id=
        "acm.all.form.CustomGroup.LaunchDialog.Controls">
      <Button Id=
        "acm.all.form.CustomGroup.LaunchDialog.Controls.Launch"
        Command="acm.all.form.CustomGroup.LaunchDialog.Controls.
          Launch.Command" Sequence="11"
        LabelText="$LocLabels:acm.all.form.CustomGroup.
          LaunchDialog.Text"
        ToolTipTitle="$LocLabels:acm.all.form.CustomGroup.
          LaunchDialog.Text"
        ToolTipDescription="$LocLabels:acm.all.form.CustomGroup.
          LaunchDialog.Text"
        TemplateAlias="isv" Image16by16="
          $webresource:acm_/images/LaunchDialog16x16.png"
        Image32by32="$webresource:acm_/images/
          LaunchDialog32x32.png" />
      </Controls>
    </Group>
  </CommandUIDefinition>
  </CustomAction>
  <CustomAction
    Id="acm.all.form.CustomGroup.MaxSize.LaunchDialog"
    Location="Mscrm.Form.{!EntityLogicalName}.MainTab.Scaling.
    _children" Sequence="1006">
  <CommandUIDefinition>
    <MaxSize Id="acm.all.form.CustomGroup.MaxSize2"
      GroupId="acm.all.form.CustomGroup.LaunchDialog"
      Sequence="16" Size="LargeLarge" />
  </CommandUIDefinition>
  </CustomAction>
</CustomActions>
```

8. Save the changes.

The XML below shows the final modified `RibbonDiffXml` for the Application Ribbon:

```
<RibbonDiffXml>
  <CustomActions>
    <CustomAction Id="acm.all.form.CustomGroup.LaunchDialogAction"
      Location="Mscrm.Form.{!EntityLogicalName}.MainTab.
      Groups._children" Sequence="1007">
      <CommandUIDefinition>
        <Group Id="acm.all.form.CustomGroup.LaunchDialog"
          Command="acm.all.form.CustomGroup.LaunchDialog.Command"
          Title="$LocLabels:acm.all.form.CustomGroup.LaunchDialog"
          Sequence="1008" Template="Mscrm.Templates.Flexible2">
          <Controls Id="acm.all.form.CustomGroup.
            LaunchDialog.Controls">
            <Button Id="acm.all.form.CustomGroup.
              LaunchDialog.Controls.Launch"
              Command="acm.all.form.CustomGroup.
                LaunchDialog.Controls.Launch.Command"
              Sequence="11"
              LabelText="$LocLabels:acm.all.form.
                CustomGroup.LaunchDialog.Text"
              ToolTipTitle="$LocLabels:acm.all.form.
                CustomGroup.LaunchDialog.Text"
              ToolTipDescription="$LocLabels:acm.all.form.
                CustomGroup.LaunchDialog.Text"
              TemplateAlias="isv" Image16by16="$webresource:
                acm_/images/LaunchDialog16x16.png"
              Image32by32="$webresource:acm_/
                images/LaunchDialog32x32.png" />
          </Controls>
        </Group>
      </CommandUIDefinition>
    </CustomAction>
    <CustomAction
      Id="acm.all.form.CustomGroup.MaxSize.LaunchDialog"
      Location="Mscrm.Form.{!EntityLogicalName}.MainTab.
      Scaling._children" Sequence="1006">
      <CommandUIDefinition>
        <MaxSize Id="acm.all.form.CustomGroup.MaxSize2"
          GroupId="acm.all.form.CustomGroup.LaunchDialog"
          Sequence="16" Size="LargeLarge" />
      </CommandUIDefinition>
    </CustomAction>
  </CustomActions>
  <Templates>
    <RibbonTemplates Id="Mscrm.Templates"></RibbonTemplates>
```

```
      </Templates>
      <CommandDefinitions>
        <CommandDefinition Id="acm.all.form.CustomGroup.
          LaunchDialog.Controls.Launch.Command">
          <EnableRules />
          <DisplayRules />
          <Actions>
            <JavaScriptFunction
              Library="$webresource:acm_/scripts/globalfunctions.js"
              FunctionName="acm_LaunchDialog"></JavaScriptFunction>
          </Actions>
        </CommandDefinition>
        <CommandDefinition Id="acm.all.form.CustomGroup.
          LaunchDialog.Command">
          <EnableRules />
          <DisplayRules>
            <DisplayRule Id="acm.all.form.CustomGroup.
              LaunchDialog.Display" />
          </DisplayRules>
          <Actions />
        </CommandDefinition>
      </CommandDefinitions>
      <RuleDefinitions>
        <TabDisplayRules />
        <DisplayRules>
          <DisplayRule Id="acm.all.form.CustomGroup.
            LaunchDialog.Display">
            <OrRule>
              <Or>
                <EntityRule EntityName="acm_airport" />
              </Or>
              <Or>
                <EntityRule EntityName="acm_compensation" />
              </Or>
              <Or>
                <EntityRule EntityName="acm_flight" />
              </Or>
              <Or>
                <EntityRule EntityName="acm_flightroute" />
              </Or>
              <Or>
                <EntityRule EntityName="contact" />
              </Or>
            </OrRule>
          </DisplayRule>
```

```
        </DisplayRules>
        <EnableRules />
      </RuleDefinitions>
      <LocLabels>
        <LocLabel Id="acm.all.form.CustomGroup.LaunchDialog">
          <Titles>
            <Title languagecode="1033"
              description="Launch ACM Dialog" />
          </Titles>
        </LocLabel>
        <LocLabel Id="acm.all.form.CustomGroup.LaunchDialog.Text">
          <Titles>
            <Title languagecode="1033"
              description="Launch ACM Dialog" />
          </Titles>
        </LocLabel>
      </LocLabels>
    </RibbonDiffXml>
```

Adding a Custom Button to the Entity Ribbon

For the ACM System, we are going to add a button to the existing Collaborate group of the Crew Member entity ribbon. The first step is to identify the IDs for Existing Items.

1. Open the `contactRibbon.xml` file using any text editing tool. The `contactRibbon.xml` file defines the ribbon for the Crew Member entity and it is the file that we exported using the tool in the SDK that we mentioned earlier this chapter.

2. Locate the following XML code in the Collaborate group for the form and the homepage grid:

Form Collaborate Group XML

```
<Group Id="Mscrm.Form.contact.MainTab.Collaborate"
       Command="Mscrm.Enabled"
       Sequence="40"
       Title="$Resources:Ribbon.HomepageGrid.MainTab.Collaborate"
       Image32by32Popup="/_imgs/ribbon/assign32.png"
       Template="Mscrm.Templates.Flexible2">
  <Controls Id="Mscrm.Form.contact.MainTab.Collaborate.Controls">
```

Homepage Grid Collaborate Group XML

```
<Group Id="Mscrm.HomepageGrid.contact.MainTab.Collaborate"
       Command="Mscrm.Enabled"
       Sequence="30"
       Title="$Resources:Ribbon.HomepageGrid.MainTab.Collaborate"
       Image32by32Popup="/_imgs/ribbon/assign32.png"
       Template="Mscrm.Templates.Flexible2">
  <Controls Id="Mscrm.HomepageGrid.contact.MainTab.Collaborate.
    Controls">
```

 Note: You will need to reference the ID values and sequence values in the subsequent steps.

3. In the `contactRibbon.xml` file, locate the Assign button definition in the Form and homepage Collaborate groups.

Form Assign Button Definition XML

```
<Button Id="Mscrm.Form.contact.Assign"
  ToolTipTitle="$Resources:Ribbon.HomepageGrid.
    MainTab.Actions.Assign"
  ToolTipDescription="$Resources(EntityPluralDisplayName):
    Ribbon.Tooltip.Assign"
  Command="Mscrm.AssignPrimaryRecord"
  Sequence="32"
  LabelText="$Resources:Ribbon.HomepageGrid.
    MainTab.Actions.Assign"
  Alt="$Resources:Ribbon.HomepageGrid.MainTab.Actions.Assign"
    Image16by16="/_imgs/ribbon/assign16.png"
    Image32by32="/_imgs/ribbon/assign32.png"
    TemplateAlias="o1" />
```

Homepage Grid Assign Button Definition XML

```
<Button Id="Mscrm.HomepageGrid.contact.Assign"
  ToolTipTitle="$Resources:Ribbon.HomepageGrid.
  MainTab.Actions.Assign"
  ToolTipDescription="$Resources(EntityPluralDisplayName):
  Ribbon.Tooltip.Assign"
  Command="Mscrm.AssignSelectedRecord"
  Sequence="40"
  LabelText="$Resources:Ribbon.HomepageGrid.
    MainTab.Actions.Assign"
  Alt="$Resources:Ribbon.HomepageGrid.MainTab.Actions.Assign"
    Image16by16="/_imgs/ribbon/assign16.png"
    Image32by32="/_imgs/ribbon/assign32.png"
    TemplateAlias="o1" />
```

Note: The Assign button in the form Collaborate group value is 32. The Assign button in the homepage grid is 40. We will use these values to figure out the location of the button in the subsequent steps.

The second step is to upload all of the components (images, JScript) that your ribbon referenced in the Web Resources. The import of the ribbon customization will fail if the referenced components are not in the Web Resources library. Please follow the steps mentioned earlier to create the following web resources:

Name	Display Name	Type
icons/TIcon16x16.png	icons/TIcon16x16.png	PNG Format
icons/TIcon16x16.png	icons/TIcon16x16.png	PNG Format
SendToOtherSystem.js	SendToOtherSystem.js	Script(JScript)

The third step is to modify the `RibbonDiffXml`. To change the entity ribbon, follow these steps:

1. Extract the exported solution ZIP file, `RibbonSolution.zip`.

2. Open the `customizations.xml` file using any text editor.

3. Locate the default `RibbonDiffXml` node, shown below for the contact entity:

```
<RibbonDiffXml>
  <CustomActions />
  <Templates>
    <RibbonTemplates Id="Mscrm.Templates"></RibbonTemplates>
  </Templates>
  <CommandDefinitions />
  <RuleDefinitions>
    <TabDisplayRules />
    <DisplayRules />
    <EnableRules />
  </RuleDefinitions>
  <LocLabels />
</RibbonDiffXml>
```

4. Edit the Rule Definition node to define the display rule and enable rules.

 Note: Enable rules are used to control when the ribbon element is enabled. Enable rules are intended to be re-used. Display rules are used to control when the ribbon elements will be displayed. You can use the same display rule for many command definitions.

```
<RuleDefinitions>
  <TabDisplayRules />
  <DisplayRules>
    <DisplayRule Id="acm.contact.form.
      FormStateNotNew.DisplayRule">
      <FormStateRule State="Create"
        InvertResult="true" />
    </DisplayRule>
    <DisplayRule Id="acm.contact.WebClient.DisplayRule">
      <CrmClientTypeRule Type="Web"/>
    </DisplayRule>
  </DisplayRules>
  <EnableRules>
    <EnableRule Id="acm.contact.WebClient.EnableRule">
      <CrmClientTypeRule Type="Web" />
    </EnableRule>
    <EnableRule Id="acm.contact.form.NotNew.EnableRule">
      <FormStateRule State="Create"
        InvertResult="true" />
    </EnableRule>
    <EnableRule Id="acm.contact.grid.OneSelected.EnableRule">
      <SelectionCountRule AppliesTo="SelectedEntity"
        Maximum="1"
        Minimum="1" />
    </EnableRule>
  </EnableRules>
</RuleDefinitions>
```

5. Edit the `LocLabels` node to set the localized labels.

```
<LocLabels>
  <LocLabel Id="acm.contact.SendToOtherSystem.LabelText">
    <Titles>
      <Title languagecode="1033"
             description="Send to Other System" />
    </Titles>
  </LocLabel>
  <LocLabel Id="acm.contact.SendToOtherSystem.ToolTip">
```

```
    <Titles>
      <Title languagecode="1033"
             description="Sends this Record to another system" />
    </Titles>
  </LocLabel>
</LocLabels>
```

6. Edit the `CommandDefinition` node to add your commands.

 Note: The `CommandDefinition` consolidates a set of enable rules and display rules, and action associated with a control.

```
<CommandDefinitions>
  <CommandDefinition Id="acm.contact.form.
    SendToOtherSystem.Command">
    <EnableRules>
      <EnableRule Id="acm.contact.WebClient.EnableRule" />
      <EnableRule Id="acm.contact.form.NotNew.EnableRule"/>
    </EnableRules>
    <DisplayRules>
      <DisplayRule Id="acm.contact.form.
        FormStateNotNew.DisplayRule" />
      <DisplayRule Id="acm.contact.WebClient.DisplayRule" />
    </DisplayRules>
    <Actions>
      <JavaScriptFunction Library="$webresource:
        acm_SendToOtherSystem.js"
        FunctionName="send" />
    </Actions>
  </CommandDefinition>
  <CommandDefinition Id="acm.contact.grid.
    SendToOtherSystem.Command">
    <EnableRules>
      <EnableRule Id="acm.contact.WebClient.EnableRule" />
      <EnableRule Id="acm.contact.grid.OneSelected.EnableRule"/>
    </EnableRules>
    <DisplayRules>
      <DisplayRule Id="acm.contact.WebClient.DisplayRule" />
    </DisplayRules>
    <Actions>
      <JavaScriptFunction Library="$webresource:
        acm_SendToOtherSystem.js"
        FunctionName="send" />
    </Actions>
  </CommandDefinition>
</CommandDefinitions>
```

7. Edit the `CustomActions` element to add your custom actions — one for each of the button that you are going to create. Use the ID values that you gathered earlier in the `contactRibbon.xml` file to set the `Location` and `Sequence` attributes to control where this button will be displayed.

Note that a custom action is a statement of how you want to change the default ribbon definition. It is evaluated and applied to the ribbon at run-time. To set the context for a custom action, you must include information about the location of the items that you want to change:

```xml
<CustomActions>
  <CustomAction Id="acm.contact.grid.
    SendToOtherSystem.CustomAction"
    Location="Mscrm.HomepageGrid.contact.
      MainTab.Collaborate.Controls._children"
    Sequence="41">
    <CommandUIDefinition>
      <Button Id="acm.contact.grid.SendToOtherSystem.Button"
        Command="acm.contact.grid.SendToOtherSystem.Command"
        LabelText="$LocLabels:acm.contact.
          SendToOtherSystem.LabelText"
        ToolTipTitle="$LocLabels:acm.contact.
          SendToOtherSystem.LabelText"
        ToolTipDescription="$LocLabels:acm.contact.
          SendToOtherSystem.ToolTip"
        TemplateAlias="o1"
        Image16by16="$webresource:acm_/icons/TIcon16x16.png"
        Image32by32="$webresource:acm_/icons/TIcon32x32.png" />
    </CommandUIDefinition>
  </CustomAction>
  <CustomAction Id="acm.contact.form.
    SendToOtherSystem.CustomAction"
    Location="Mscrm.Form.contact.MainTab.
    Collaborate.Controls._children"
    Sequence="33">
    <CommandUIDefinition>
      <Button Id="acm.contact.form.SendToOtherSystem.Button"
        Command="acm.contact.form.SendToOtherSystem.Command"
        LabelText="$LocLabels:acm.contact.
          SendToOtherSystem.LabelText"
        ToolTipTitle="$LocLabels:acm.contact.
          SendToOtherSystem.LabelText"
        ToolTipDescription="$LocLabels:acm.contact.
          SendToOtherSystem.ToolTip"
        TemplateAlias="o1"
        Image16by16="$webresource:acm_/icons/TIcon16x16.png"
        Image32by32="$webresource:acm_/icons/TIcon32x32.png" />
    </CommandUIDefinition>
  </CustomAction>
</CustomActions>
```

8. Save the changes.

9. Compress the modified customization file for the solution.

10. Import and publish the solution.

The XML below shows the final modified `RibbonDiffXml` for the Crew Member entity:

```
<RibbonDiffXml>
  <CustomActions>
  <CustomAction Id="acm.contact.grid.SendToOtherSystem.
CustomAction"
    Location="Mscrm.HomepageGrid.contact.MainTab.
    Collaborate.Controls._children"
    Sequence="41">
    <CommandUIDefinition>
      <Button Id="acm.contact.grid.SendToOtherSystem.Button"
        Command="acm.contact.grid.SendToOtherSystem.Command"
        LabelText="$LocLabels:acm.contact.
          SendToOtherSystem.LabelText"
        ToolTipTitle="$LocLabels:acm.contact.
          SendToOtherSystem.LabelText"
        ToolTipDescription="$LocLabels:acm.contact.
          SendToOtherSystem.ToolTip"
        TemplateAlias="o1"
        Image16by16="$webresource:acm_/icons/TIcon16x16.png"
        Image32by32="$webresource:acm_/icons/TIcon32x32.png" />
    </CommandUIDefinition>
  </CustomAction>
  <CustomAction Id="acm.contact.form.SendToOtherSystem.
CustomAction"
    Location="Mscrm.Form.contact.MainTab.Collaborate.
    Controls._children"
    Sequence="33">
    <CommandUIDefinition>
      <Button Id="acm.contact.form.SendToOtherSystem.Button"
        Command="acm.contact.form.SendToOtherSystem.Command"
        LabelText="$LocLabels:acm.contact.
          SendToOtherSystem.LabelText"
        ToolTipTitle="$LocLabels:acm.contact.
          SendToOtherSystem.LabelText"
        ToolTipDescription="$LocLabels:acm.contact.
          SendToOtherSystem.ToolTip"
        TemplateAlias="o1"
        Image16by16="$webresource:acm_/icons/TIcon16x16.png"
        Image32by32="$webresource:acm_/icons/TIcon32x32.png" />
    </CommandUIDefinition>
  </CustomAction>
```

```
    </CustomActions>

    <Templates>
      <RibbonTemplates Id="Mscrm.Templates"></RibbonTemplates>
    </Templates>

<CommandDefinitions>
    <CommandDefinition Id="acm.contact.form.SendToOtherSystem.
Command">
      <EnableRules>
        <EnableRule Id="acm.contact.WebClient.EnableRule" />
        <EnableRule Id="acm.contact.form.NotNew.EnableRule"/>
      </EnableRules>
      <DisplayRules>
        <DisplayRule Id="acm.contact.form.
          FormStateNotNew.DisplayRule" />
        <DisplayRule Id="acm.contact.WebClient.DisplayRule" />
      </DisplayRules>
      <Actions>
        <JavaScriptFunction Library="$webresource:
          acm_SendToOtherSystem.js"
          FunctionName="send" />
      </Actions>
    </CommandDefinition>
    <CommandDefinition Id="acm.contact.grid.SendToOtherSystem.
Command">
      <EnableRules>
        <EnableRule Id="acm.contact.WebClient.EnableRule" />
        <EnableRule Id="acm.contact.grid.OneSelected.EnableRule"/>
      </EnableRules>
      <DisplayRules>
        <DisplayRule Id="acm.contact.WebClient.DisplayRule" />
      </DisplayRules>
      <Actions>
        <JavaScriptFunction Library=
          "$webresource:acm_SendToOtherSystem.js"
          FunctionName="send" />
      </Actions>
    </CommandDefinition>
</CommandDefinitions>

    <RuleDefinitions>
      <TabDisplayRules />
      <DisplayRules />
      <EnableRules />
```

```xml
<RuleDefinitions>
  <TabDisplayRules />
  <DisplayRules>
    <DisplayRule Id="acm.contact.form.FormStateNotNew.
DisplayRule">
      <FormStateRule State="Create"
                     InvertResult="true" />
    </DisplayRule>
    <DisplayRule Id="acm.contact.WebClient.DisplayRule">
      <CrmClientTypeRule Type="Web"/>
    </DisplayRule>
  </DisplayRules>
  <EnableRules>
    <EnableRule Id="acm.contact.WebClient.EnableRule">
      <CrmClientTypeRule Type="Web" />
    </EnableRule>
    <EnableRule Id="acm.contact.form.NotNew.EnableRule">
      <FormStateRule State="Create"
                     InvertResult="true" />
    </EnableRule>
    <EnableRule Id="acm.contact.grid.OneSelected.EnableRule">
      <SelectionCountRule AppliesTo="SelectedEntity"
                          Maximum="1"
                          Minimum="1" />
    </EnableRule>
  </EnableRules>
</RuleDefinitions>

  <LocLabels>
  <LocLabel Id="acm.contact.SendToOtherSystem.LabelText">
    <Titles>
      <Title languagecode="1033"
             description="Send to Other System" />
    </Titles>
  </LocLabel>
  <LocLabel Id="acm.contact.SendToOtherSystem.ToolTip">
    <Titles>
      <Title languagecode="1033"
             description="Sends this Record to another system" />
    </Titles>
  </LocLabel>
</LocLabels>
</RibbonDiffXml>
```

Hiding a Ribbon element

To hide a ribbon element, follow the same steps above to export the ribbon. Then locate the Location and the ID of the control that you want to hide from the exported `<entity>Ribbon.xml`. Finally, specify the control that you want to hide, in the `CustomActions` area, as shown in the sample code below:

Hide Data Group on the Crew Member Entity Ribbon

```
<RibbonDiffXml>
  <CustomActions >
    <HideCustomAction
      Location="Mscrm.HomepageGrid.contact.MainTab.ExportData"
      HideActionId="Sample.HomepageGrid.contact.MainTab.
      ExportData.HideAction" />
  </CustomActions>
  <Templates>
    <RibbonTemplates Id="Mscrm.Templates">
    </RibbonTemplates>
  </Templates>
  <CommandDefinitions />
  <RuleDefinitions>
    <TabDisplayRules />
    <DisplayRules />
    <EnableRules />
  </RuleDefinitions>
  <LocLabels />
</RibbonDiffXml>
```

Summary

There you go! We have covered the basics of customizing the SiteMap and the Ribbon. The Ribbon is new in Microsoft Dynamics CRM 2011 and you need a lot of practice to master ribbon customization. Once you master the different components in the ribbon definition, there's a lot more things that you can do with CRM navigation, when compared to Microsoft Dynamics CRM 4.0.

There are also a few unofficial SiteMap and Ribbon editor tools developed by the community, so you can try it out. In the next chapter, we are going to look at how to package the entire ACM system that we have built.

10
Packaging It Up

At this point of the book, we have completed building different components of the Airline Compensation Management System (ACM). Now we need to package the solution for deployment into other environments or the Dynamics Marketplace. Microsoft Dynamics CRM 2011 provides a framework upon which custom business applications can be built. It introduced the concept of a "solution" by providing full support for creating, trying, installing, upgrading, and deleting business applications that run on the Dynamics CRM 2011 framework. In this chapter, we are going to cover solutions in detail:

- What's new in CRM 2011?
- What is a solution?
- Packaging the ACM solution
- What is the difference between unmanaged and managed solutions?
- Exporting a solution

What is new in CRM 2011?

In the previous version of Dynamics CRM, we are faced with many challenges when we are going to package the final solution for deployment, such as overwriting customer changes, no dependency tracking, versioning, or separate deployment packages for the various artifacts. Most people are still having challenges moving the solution from a development environment to a staging environment, and from a staging environment to a production environment. The deployment story for CRM was poor. The traditional development paradigm, such as contiguous integration and build automation, cannot be used with Microsoft Dynamics CRM. With the previous version of CRM, most of the deployments are manual unless you write your own automatic deployment engine. The deployment steps are very trivial, and administrators have export and import customizations, and register plugins and workflow assemblies. It is a very time-consuming process.

Microsoft Dynamics CRM 2011 has improved the deployment story. However, it is still not perfect because its deployment is still not the same as the traditional .NET web application, where developers can build a single installation package for the deployment administrators to deploy. Microsoft Dynamics CRM 2011 introduced a new concept called a 'solution'. A solution is a container of components designated to provide specific business functionality, and that is authored, packaged, and maintained as a single unit of software. The goal it is trying to accomplish is that we build our solution once and deploy it everywhere it is needed, as indicated in the following screenshot:

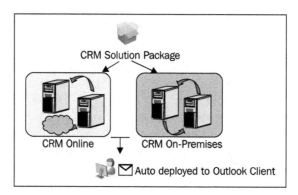

What is a solution? Let's take a look at a solution in detail.

Solution

A solution is built using the Microsoft Dynamics CRM interfaces, and is hosted inside the CRM framework. It is also run inside the CRM framework. The valid components that can be included in the solution are the following:

- Data Model
    - ° Entity and Attribute Definitions
    - ° Option Sets
    - ° One to Many Relationships
    - ° Many to Many Relationships

- Modifications to the CRM User Interface
  - Forms and Views
  - Application Ribbons
  - Entity Ribbons
  - Site Map
  - Charts
- Web Resources
  - Images and Icons
  - HTML Pages
  - Style Sheets
  - JavaScript
  - Silverlight Controls
  - XML Files
- Processes and Code
  - Workflow Definitions
  - Dialog Definitions
  - Custom Plug-in and Workflow Assemblies
- Analytics
  - Dashboards
  - Reports
- Templates
  - Article Templates
  - Contract Templates
  - Email Templates
  - Mail Merge Templates
- Security
  - Security Roles
  - Field Security Profiles

A solution may contain a completely new vertical solution or enhancements to existing product functionality. A solution is the software unit that allows developers to create, transport, and maintain business solutions that run on top of the CRM framework. In addition to allowing you to group components, a solution also provides additional metadata to identify the functionality that you are providing. The following table identifies the key metadata attributes of a solution:

Attributes	Description
Display Name	Friendly name to identify the solution
Name	Unique name that identifies the solution
Version	User-specified number that indicates the revision of the solution
Description	Text explaining what the solution does
Solution Publisher	Author of the solution
Configuration Page	Instructions for installing the solution

To create a solution, navigate to the **Settings** area and then click on **Solutions** under the **Customization** tab. Click on the **New** button to create a new solution, as shown in the following screenshot:

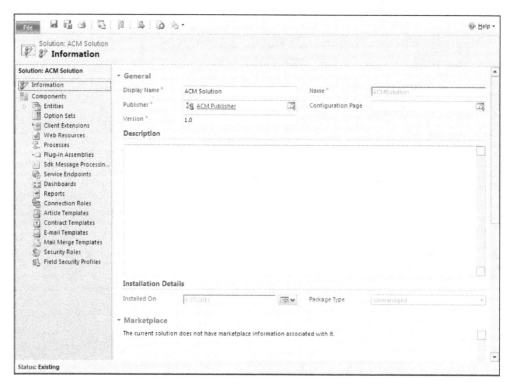

On the Solution form, populate the **Display Name**, **Publisher**, and **Version** fields, and then click the **Save** button to create the solution.

Solution Publisher

Each solution has a publisher associated with it. A solution publisher represents the author of a solution. The following table identifies the key metadata attribute of a Solution Publisher:

Attributes	Description
Display Name	Friendly name to identify the solution publisher
Unique Name	Unique name to identify the solution publisher
Customization Prefix	Whenever new components are created in the system, the system uses the prefix of the corresponding publisher to namespace the component
Numeric Prefix	Used for Option Sets
Address	Publisher's address
Web Site Address	URL for the publisher

To create a publisher, navigate to the **Settings** area, click on **Customizations** under the **Customization** tab, and then click on **Publishers**. Click on the **New** button to create a new publisher, as shown in the following screenshot:

On the Publisher form, populate the **Display Name**, **Prefix**, and **Option Value Prefix** fields, and then click the **Save** button to create the **Publisher**.

Packing an ACM Solution

Once the solution is created, we can now add the related ACM components to this solution. Let's do a walk through of how to add entities to the solution. To add the rest of the components, we can follow similar steps.

Entities

To add entities to the solution, navigate to the **Entities** area. We can perform the following actions in this area, from the grid toolbar in this section, as shown:

- Create New Entity
- Add Existing Entities
- Delete Entities
- Remove Entities
- Show Dependencies
- Add Required Components
- Managed Properties

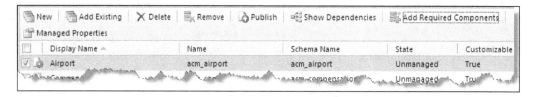

For our ACM solution, we are going to add the following entities, as shown:

- Airport
- Compensation
- Crew Member
- Flight
- Flight Route

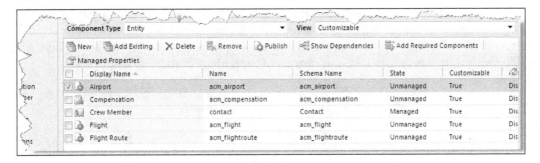

If we want to include all of the entities that the specific entity is related to, select the entity in the solution, then click on the **Add Required Components** button on the grid toolbar.

Following similar steps to those outlined above, add OptionSets, Web Resources, Plug-ins, Processes, Reports, and Dashboards to the solution for the ACM system.

Difference between Unmanaged and Managed Solutions

Solutions can be packaged as "unmanaged" or as "managed". Having a good understanding of the capabilities and limitations of each package type is very important for developers and CRM administrators, as it has deep implications on the way that CRM 2011 processes components. Let's take a look at the two different package types in detail.

Unmanaged

It doesn't matter how you are creating the initial solution, every newly-solution is unmanaged. The new solution is just a container that holds references to components in the system. Adding components to the solution is as simple as selecting from any existing components, or creating new components from the context of the solution. Unmanaged solutions only have a reference to components in the system, and do not have a copy of a component. Multiple unmanaged solutions can have a reference to the same component, and changes made to the component will be visible in all other solutions regardless, of the solution that we performed the changes on. Exporting any solution that contains the component will export all of the changes made, irrespective of which unmanaged solution the changes were performed on. The following figure provides a visual representation of an unmanaged solution:

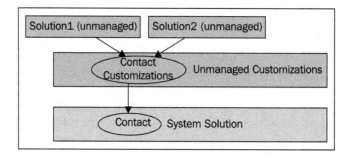

Any time we need to perform direct modifications to the solution metadata, or add or remove components, we will need to do so on the unmanaged solution.

Whenever we need to transport the solution from one development environment to another environment, and we intend to perform additional changes to the solution, we need to transport it as unmanaged. Importing an unmanaged solution is similar to how Microsoft Dynamics CRM 4.0 works, and always overwrites the components that it touches. When deleting an unmanaged solution, only the container is deleted, and the components will remain in the system. So in other words, components installed by an unmanaged solution cannot be uninstalled.

Managed

Managed solutions were designed for the final distribution of components. After initial development is done and the solution is ready to be consumed by customers we need to export it as managed. When a solution is exported as managed and subsequently imported in a different organization, the definition of the solution is locked and components cannot be added or removed. Components can still be customized, but customizations need to be carried out in an unmanaged solution. All changes are tracked as customizations performed "on top" of the solution:

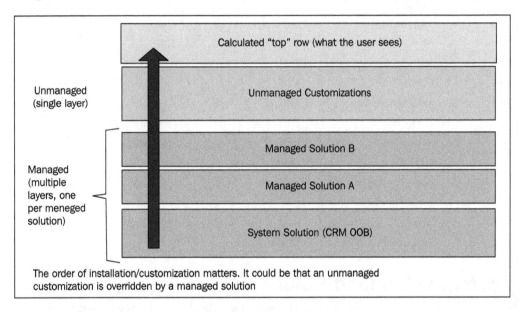

The layering approach allows solutions to be built on top of each other, and also provides flexibility for end-customers to tailor the solution to fit their needs.

Another benefit of managed solutions is that they can be uninstalled. To uninstall a managed solution, we just need to delete the solution. Deleting a managed solution will delete all of its components, and will roll back any changes that were performed by the solution.

When exporting a solution as managed, Microsoft Dynamics CRM 2011 automatically figures out the items should be included in the customization. Some components in the solution file contain the delta whereas some components contain everything. CRM automatically figures out the appropriate action when importing a managed solution, some components get the delta whereas some components get overwritten. The following table shows the import behaviors for each of the solution components:

Component	Export Behavior	Import Behavior
Entity		
Attributes	Delta	Delta
Forms	Delta	Delta
Views	Full	Overwritten
Charts	Full	Overwritten
Web Resources	Full	Isolated
Reports	Full	Overwritten
Processes	Full	Overwritten
Global Option Sets	Delta	Delta
Security Roles	Full	Overwritten
Field Security Profile	Full	Overwritten
Site Map	Full	Overwritten
Application Ribbon	Delta	Delta

Updating Managed Solutions

Whenever we deploy an update to a managed solution, the changes are deployed to the corresponding layer, which allows the system to preserve customizations instead of blowing them. The system will automatically detect that the solution is already installed in the system and prompt us to confirm the installation of the update. We have the choice to preserve the existing customizations or replace them.

The solutions framework is optimized to handle updates to full solutions. Creating an update for a solution can be as simple as changing the version number of the solution in the development environment, performing the changes, packaging the solution, and delivering it to the customer. When we apply the update, the solutions framework will deploy the update and do its best to preserve the existing customizations. This approach works just fine when solutions have been properly modularized, but it can become a challenge for solutions that have a large number of components and only a small subset of those need to be mandatorily updated. This is commonly known as a "patch".

The best approach to "patch" a solution is to:

1. Create another solution in the same organization that contains the solution to be patched. Let's call it the "patch" solution. The solution publisher used to create the patch solution must be exactly the same as the one used to create the original solution, otherwise the update might be prevented during import due to managed properties (see the managed properties section).

2. In the patch solution, only include (add existing) the components that need to be updated.

3. Perform the changes and package the update as a managed solution.

4. Deliver the patch to the customer.

The "patch" approach allows us to deliver a subset of changes to our customers and will also allow us to uninstall the patch if something goes wrong. Do note that any customizations performed on the components being updated will be lost with this approach, but that should be ok as the components need to be mandatorily updated.

Conflict resolution

When two or more solutions perform changes to the same component, the system can resolve the conflict by using one of the following strategies:

- **Merge**: User interface components (Ribbons, Forms, and Sitemap) have the capability to merge. The system starts with the system solution and continues with any subsequent solutions installed on top of this, plus any additional customizations. At each step the system merges the changes, and what we see at run-time is the result of the merge.

- **Last one wins**: As the name implies, with this resolution, which is applicable to all components except the ones that support merging capabilities, the "top" change is the one that wins. For example, if multiple solutions rename an entity, what we will see at run-time is the last rename. The "top" change doesn't necessarily imply the last solution updated. If we install a solution update but chose to "preserve" the customizations, the top row will still be the customizations and not the contents of the update.

The following diagram provides a visual representation of conflict solution in Microsoft Dynamics CRM 2011:

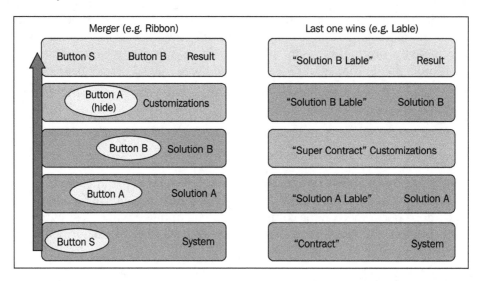

If developers need to deploy a "patch" that affects only a subset of components and they want to ensure that the changes in the patch are effective, they can opt to deliver the patch as a different solution, but with the same publisher.

Managed properties

Most components that ship with CRM 2011 are customizable. For example, we can add or remove attributes from a specific entity, change the display strings of a particular object, change the user interface, and so on. Sometimes, however, certain behaviors of a component need to be restricted to prevent changes that would "break" the system, or to facilitate support/maintenance of the component in the future. For example allowing customers to delete key components on the system would lead to a malfunction. Developers creating CRM solutions face a similar challenge. We could inadvertently change or remove components that break the solution.

Managed properties provide granular control over specific aspects of a component. The most evident benefit of managed properties is that they allow developers to selectively restrict the customizability of a component. All that developers have to do is to set the value corresponding to the managed property to true or false, as indicated in the following screenshot:

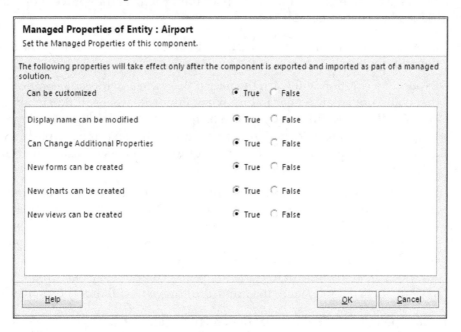

Once a solution is installed as managed, the system will enforce the behavior specified by managed properties. Additionally, the system will prevent changing the value of the managed property itself. The only exception is the solution import. During import of a solution, the system matches the solution publisher specified in the package with the solution publisher on the target system, and if they match the system allows the value of the managed properties to be changed. However, once an operation is allowed and we perform the operation, the system will not allow the update of a managed property to make it more restrictive, as this could lead to an inconsistent state.

Dependency tracking

The solutions framework automatically tracks dependencies across components. Every core operation (create/update/delete) on a component automatically calculates its dependencies to other components in the system. The dependency information is used to maintain the integrity of the system, and to prevent operations that would lead to an inconsistent state.

- Deletion of a component will be prevented if other components in the system depend upon it.

- Export of a solution will warn the user if there are any missing components that could potentially cause failure when importing that solution in another system. Warnings during export can be ignored if the solution developer is purposely building a dependency on a "base" solution (for example, they are building on top of a solution, and require customers to install the base solution first).

- Import of a solution will fail if all required components are not contained in the solution and also don't exist in the target system. Additionally, when importing a managed solution, all required components must match the package type of the solution; in other words a component in a managed solution can only depend on another managed component (same or distinct solution). If, at the time of import, a required component exists on the target system but is not managed, the import routine will still report it as missing.

An important point to highlight is that dependencies are version agnostic. CRM 2011 tracks dependencies across components using their unique identifiers (unique name or GUID), which doesn't include any versioning information.

Export and Import Solution

Now that we have developed the ACM solution in our development workspace, let's go ahead and export it and then import it to CRM Online.

Exporting a solution

Go to **ACM** | **Settings** | **Solutions**, double-click on the **ACM Solution** to open it, and then click on **Export Solution** on the toolbar. The **Publish Customizations** form will open. In order to include the latest customizations, it's recommended to publish all customizations before exporting the solution. To publish all customizations, simply click on the **Publish All Customizations** button. Then click **Next**.

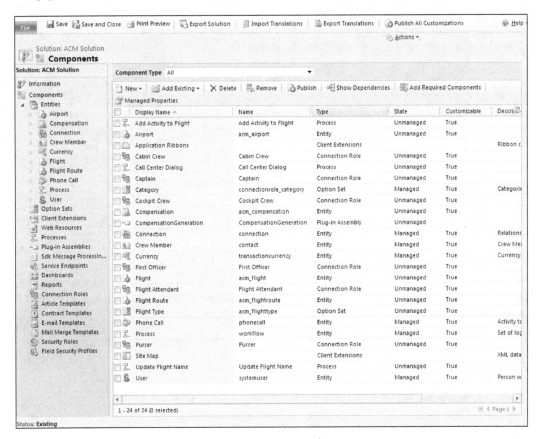

Microsoft Dynamics CRM 2011 has dependency tracking built into the product. If it detects a missing component, the **Missing Required Components** screen will tell us what is missing from this solution, as shown in the next screenshot. We can then go back and add the missing components to the solution and then export the solution again.

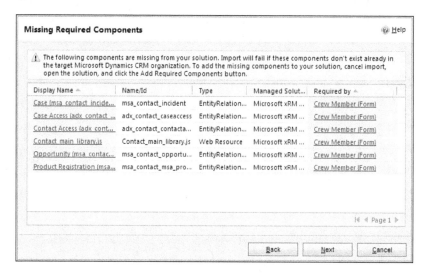

On the **Export System Settings** (**Advanced**) screen, as shown in the following screenshot, select the setting that you want to export. It is recommended that you do not export the system settings (**Calendar**, **Customization**, **E-mail tracking**, **General**, **Marketing**, **Outlook Synchronization**):

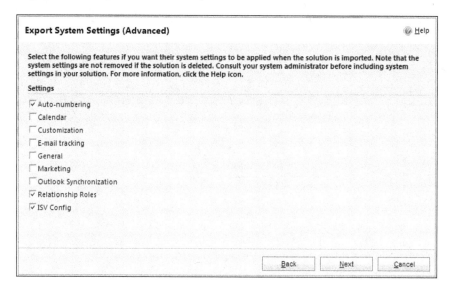

On the **Package Type** screen, as indicated in the following screenshot, export the solution as a managed solution, by selecting **Managed**. Next, click the **Export** button to export the solution.

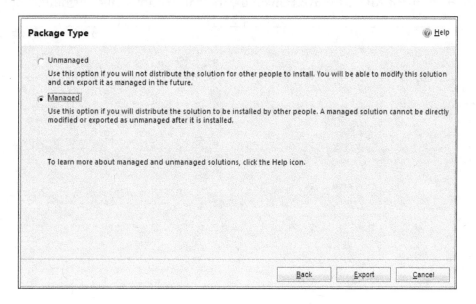

Importing a solution

To import the solution to CRM Online, go to **ACM | Settings | Solutions**, and then click on **Import Solution** on the toolbar. First of all, import the **Customer Portal** solution, and then import the managed ACM solution.

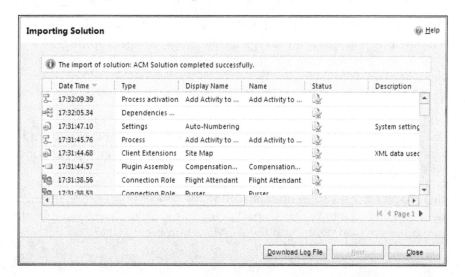

Click **Close** and then refresh the page. You will see both solutions are applied on CRM Online.

Click the **Publish All Customization** on the toolbar to publish the customizations.

As a result, all customizations, including Processes and Plug-ins, are imported. However, note that you still need to register the Steps/Images for Plug-ins.

Summary

Microsoft Dynamics CRM 2011 provides new way for us to package our customization into a solution. It allows us to transport our solution easily and, most importantly, it protects us by allowing us to package our customization in a managed solution, where it protects our intellectual property.

I hope this chapter helps you in understanding the concept of solution in Microsoft Dynamics CRM 2011. Once we finish packaging our solution, we can deploy the solution to other environments, and the ACM system is complete.

Index

R

referencing ways, web resources. *See* **web resources, referencing ways**
relationship 27
relative URL
  using, for web resource referencing 86
ResourceId attribute 213
REST endpoint
  about 98
  using, for creating Crew Member 99
  using, for deleting Crew Member 102
  using, for retrieving Crew Member 100
  using, for updating Crew Member 101, 102
REST(Representational State Transfer) 98
ribbon definition
  exporting 218
RibbonDiffXml 218
RibbonDiffXml definition 219
RibbonDiffXml node 233
ribbon element
  hiding 240
ribbon export tool
  location 218
ribbons
  Custom Button, adding to entity ribbon 231-239
  entity ribbons 219
  form ribbons 221
  grid ribbons 220
  ribbon definitions, exporting 222, 224
  ribbon element, hiding 240
  sub grid ribbons 221
  To Button, adding to application ribbon 224-229
  working with 222

S

SaaS (Software-as-a-Service) 183
Sales Activity Dashboard 176
Sales Performance Dashboard 176
Script (JScript) 83
SDK Assemblies. *See* **CRM SDK Assemblies**
security, plug-ins 120
security roles, ACM system
  ACM Manager Role 55

ACM Schedulers Role 55
CRM Administrator Role 55
Flight Crew Role 55
security settings, SharePoint 162
security structure, ACM system 55, 56
Server Environment
  setting up, on VM 10
set aggregations
  Average (Avg) 172
  Count 172
  Maximum (Max) 172
  Minimum (Min) 172
  Sum 172
SharePoint 2010 Online 184
SharePoint 2010 Server
  installing 12
  setting up 12
  SharePoint web application, creating 12, 13
SharePoint integration
  about 147, 150
  Document ID 161
  document management settings 151, 152
  Document Set 160
  Document View 161
  flowchart 150
  security settings 162
  setting up 147
  SharePoint sites 153
  working 150
SharePoint integration, setting up
  CRM List Component 148
  CRM List Component, installing 149
  SharePoint 2010 site collection, creating 147, 148
SharePoint Management Console 149
SharePoint security
  about 162
  URL 162
SharePoint site
  creating 153
  document location, adding 154-156
SharePoint site collection
  about 147
  creating 147
  URL 147
SharePoint Sites and Document Locations
  hierarchy 155
Silverlight
  SOAP endpoint, using with 98

Thank you for buying
Microsoft Dynamics CRM 2011 New Features

About Packt Publishing

Packt, pronounced 'packed', published its first book "Mastering phpMyAdmin for Effective MySQL Management" in April 2004 and subsequently continued to specialize in publishing highly focused books on specific technologies and solutions.

Our books and publications share the experiences of your fellow IT professionals in adapting and customizing today's systems, applications, and frameworks. Our solution based books give you the knowledge and power to customize the software and technologies you're using to get the job done. Packt books are more specific and less general than the IT books you have seen in the past. Our unique business model allows us to bring you more focused information, giving you more of what you need to know, and less of what you don't.

Packt is a modern, yet unique publishing company, which focuses on producing quality, cutting-edge books for communities of developers, administrators, and newbies alike. For more information, please visit our website: www.packtpub.com.

About Packt Enterprise

In 2010, Packt launched two new brands, Packt Enterprise and Packt Open Source, in order to continue its focus on specialization. This book is part of the Packt Enterprise brand, home to books published on enterprise software – software created by major vendors, including (but not limited to) IBM, Microsoft and Oracle, often for use in other corporations. Its titles will offer information relevant to a range of users of this software, including administrators, developers, architects, and end users.

Writing for Packt

We welcome all inquiries from people who are interested in authoring. Book proposals should be sent to author@packtpub.com. If your book idea is still at an early stage and you would like to discuss it first before writing a formal book proposal, contact us; one of our commissioning editors will get in touch with you.

We're not just looking for published authors; if you have strong technical skills but no writing experience, our experienced editors can help you develop a writing career, or simply get some additional reward for your expertise.

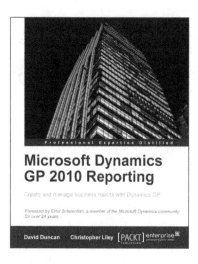

Microsoft Dynamics GP 2010 Reporting

ISBN: 978-1-84968-218-3   Paperback: 360 pages

Create and manage business reports with Dynamics GP

1. Identify the major reporting challenges facing your organization and select the most effective reporting tool to meet those challenges

2. Empower users from top to bottom in your organization to create their own reports

3. Go beyond basic reporting by providing true business intelligence for your organization

4. Discover how to use reporting tools to mine and analyze your Dynamics GP data for maximum competitive advantage

Microsoft Dynamics GP 2010 Cookbook

ISBN: 978-1-849680-42-4   Paperback: 324 pages

Solve real-world Dynamics GP problems with over 100 immediately usable and incredibly effective recipes

1. Discover how to solve real-world Dynamics GP problems with immediately useable recipes

2. Follow carefully organized sequences of instructions along with screenshots

3. Understand the various tips and tricks to master Dynamics GP, improve your system's stability, and enable you to get work done faster

Please check **www.PacktPub.com** for information on our titles

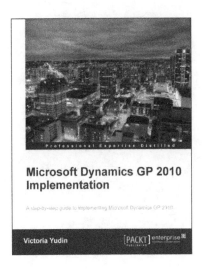

Microsoft Dynamics GP 2010 Implementation

ISBN: 978-1-84968-032-5   Paperback: 376 pages

A step-by-step guide to implementing Microsoft Dynamics GP 2010

1. Master how to implement Microsoft Dynamics GP 2010 with real world examples and guidance from a Microsoft Dynamics GP MVP

2. Understand how to install Microsoft Dynamics GP 2010 and related applications, following detailed, step-by-step instructions

3. Learn how to set-up the core Microsoft Dynamics GP modules effectively

4. Discover the additional tools available from Microsoft for Dynamics GP

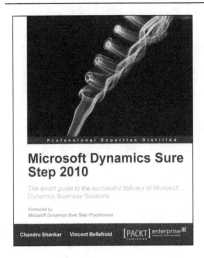

Microsoft Dynamics Sure Step 2010

ISBN: 978-1-84968-110-0   Paperback: 360 pages

The smart guide to the successful delivery of Microsoft Dynamics Business Solutions

1. Learn how to effectively use Microsoft Dynamics Sure Step to implement the right Dynamics business solution with quality, on-time and on-budget results

2. Leverage the Decision Accelerator offerings in Microsoft Dynamics Sure Step to create consistent selling motions while helping your customer ascertain the best solution to fit their requirements

Please check **www.PacktPub.com** for information on our titles

www.ingramcontent.com/pod-product-compliance
Lightning Source LLC
LaVergne TN
LVHW062309060326
832902LV00013B/2122